A Vintner's Guide to *Red Wine*

Also by Joy Sterling

A Cultivated Life

*Vintage Feasting**

Vineyard: A Year in the Life of California's Wine Country

*Available from Pocket Books

A Vintner's Guide to Red Wine

What to Buy and What to Drink in the Year 2000

Joy Sterling

POCKET BOOKS
NEW YORK LONDON TORONTO SYDNEY TOKYO SINGAPORE

An *Original* Publication of POCKET BOOKS

POCKET BOOKS, a division of Simon & Schuster Inc.
1230 Avenue of the Americas, New York, NY 10020

Library of Congress Cataloging-in-Publication Data

Sterling, Joy.
A vintner's guide to red wine : what to buy and what to drink in the year 2000 / Joy Sterling.
p. cm.
ISBN: 0-671-01143-X
1. Wine and wine making. I. Title. II. Title: Red wine.
TP548.S722 1999
641.2'223–dc21 99-37429
CIP

First Pocket Books trade paperback printing October 1999

10 9 8 7 6 5 4 3 2 1

Cover design and illustration by Jeanne M. Lee
Designed by Joseph Rutt

Printed in the U.S.A.

For family and friends

Acknowledgments

My most sincere thanks to my husband Forrest Tancer, my parents Audrey and Barry Sterling, my brother Laurence Sterling, Dan Green, Emily Bestler, and my great friends Joseph Bastianich, Maralee Beck, Ann Berta, Larry Brooks, Craig Camp, Bill Crawford, Dean Gold, David Graves, John Haeger, Herman Isacs III, James Jackson, Josh Jensen, Fuad Jezzini, Andy Katz, J.B. Meaders, Denman Moody, David Munksgard, Charlie Palmer, John Roenigk, Richard Sanford, Piero Selvaggio, Larry Stone, Steve Wallace, Josh Wesson, and Susan Van Koughnett who helped me with research.

Contents

INTRODUCTION
My Opinions; Personal Bias; Why Red Wine?; Vineyards, Wineries, and Winemakers
1

CALIFORNIA CABERNET
Decisions, Decisions; Personal Recommendations; Comparisons with Bordeaux; Vintage Chart; When to Drink; Food and Wine Pairings
15

CALIFORNIA AND OREGON PINOT NOIR
The Grape; Personal Recommendations; Comparisons with Burgundy; Vintage Chart; When to Drink; Food and Wine Pairings
38

MERLOT, MERLOT, MERLOT
High Brow, Low Brow; Personal Recommendations; Comparisons with Bordeaux; When to Drink; Vintage Chart; Food and Wine Pairings
57

ZINFANDEL
All-American; Personal Recommendations; Vintage Chart; When to Drink; Food and Wine Pairings
67

CALIFORNIA SYRAH
Character of the Grape; Personal Recommendations; When to Drink; Comparisons with France and Australia; Vintage Chart; Food and Wine Pairings
75

CALIFORNIA ITALIAN
History: Sangiovese, Nebbiolo, Barbera, and Dolcetto; Sangiovese History; Personal Recommendations for Sangiovese; When to Drink Sangiovese; Comparisons of California Sangiovese with Tuscan Wines; Food and Sangiovese Wine Pairings; Nebbiolo History; When to Drink Nebbiolo; Food and Nebbiolo Wine Pairings; Barbera History; Dolcetto History
84

ROSÉS
The Height of Sophistication; Personal Recommendations; When to Drink; Food and Wine Pairings
95

EPILOGUE
Looking Forward
101

INDEX
103

A Vintner's Guide to *Red Wine*

Introduction

MY OPINIONS

This is a book for lovers of red wine, written for other wine enthusiasts who want to know what I like. The result is an informative companion full of practical advice and personal opinions that you can take with you into a store or on a trip. It begins with a short essay on red wine, but the meat and potatoes is a buying guide to each type of red, organized by the grapes or a particular grouping, like Rosés—the way wine lists and stores are usually laid out. My hope is to help you decide what you want to have in your glass as we approach the turn of the millennium.

This book covers Cabernet Sauvignon, Pinot Noir, Merlot, Zinfandel, Syrah, California-Italian varietals, and dry Rosés—primarily from California, though Oregon and Washington are given their full due. Fine wine is now produced in 40 states—you can go to a wine festival somewhere in America almost every weekend of the year, and in each state there are individual producers who stand out, like Horton Cellars Winery in Virginia and Palmer Vineyards in New York—but 90 percent of America's wine comes from California. Oregon has captured the imagination for Pinot Noir, and Washington State, which excels at Merlot, recently surpassed New York in producing the second highest volume.

As a Californian, I naturally start with the grapes. I try to describe the pleasures of each varietal and explore such topics as the differences between California

Pinot Noir and Burgundy, why you spend a fortune on Burgundy when you can get *really* good California Pinot Noir more consistently, for far less money, how Sonoma Pinot Noir differs from Central Coast, and how Oregon fits into the picture. Reading is fun, but reading and drinking is better, so maybe you should have a glass in hand.

Most American vintners feel their wines shouldn't have to withstand comparisons with Europe, Australia, or Chile—comparisons as odious as mixing apples and oranges. And yes, it's true there are so many different regions, styles, and other variables that it's hard to make sweeping statements. However, I feel that side-stepping the obvious, basic questions is like a waiter's telling you everything on the menu is good—it's not very useful.

Then, for each varietal, I talk about the producers I tend to follow, famous vineyards, choice vintages, what to drink now, and the best combinations with food. My personal recommendations fall into three categories: expensive (which for me is over $25), moderate ($12 to $25), and inexpensive (under $12). I have been guided above all by wines that make me smile.

The book is geared to one year—what to buy and what to drink in 2000—because many wine guides are outdated by the time they are published. I have included vintage charts, which are as subjective as everything else about wine. And I have concentrated on the foods my family loves to eat. You will find that I like all wines with roast chicken.

PERSONAL BIAS

I feel that anyone who proffers an opinion should disclose any and all prejudices. So, before we go another step, there are certain things you should know about me.

First of all, I am completely biased. Iron Horse Vineyards, my family's winery, is always my first choice. My whole life and everyone I love are wrapped up in Iron Horse. My husband, Forrest Tancer, manages the vineyards and is the chief winemaker. I am in charge of sales, marketing, and public relations. My parents, my brother and sister-in-law, their children, and Forrest and I all live on the vineyard. The style of our wines is dictated by the land, but there's no doubt that ingredient X in the best wines is the personality of the people behind them.

I am a fifth-generation Californian, naturally chauvinistic, and tend to think of the Golden State as a country unto itself. If spun off, California would rank as the seventh largest economy in the world, right after Italy.

I'm not particularly fond of Merlot. I've tasted the Arrowood Merlot, which everyone fights over, next to Arrowood's excellent Cabernet, and I just don't get it.

Pinot Noir is my favorite red-wine grape.

I am a born contrarian. On many issues, you will see the entire wine trade going one way and one short blonde headed in the opposite direction.

My preferred style is dry, soft, luscious, and fruity. I like old, beautifully cellared Cabernets with that "ten-year magic" in an age when 95 percent of all wine is consumed the day it is purchased. Most of the time, I favor California Cabernet over Bordeaux—unless it's an exceptional vintage. To me, a Bordeaux dinner with 1994, 1981, 1979, and 1971 First Growths (which are the top Bordeaux vineyards—Chateaux Lafite-Rothschild, Latour, Margaux, Mouton-Rothschild, and Haut-Brion)—which each retail for well over $100 a bottle—is strictly educational. These are vintages you would drink if that were the price you could afford. You could forgive the '94s for being too young, and the older wines did indeed have structure. Yes, they are long lived, but they seemed thin, lacking in fruit, and bitter in the finish. My conclusion is not that Château Haut-Brion is slipping but that my palate is more attuned to California. I love the fruit.

I can be as narrow-minded about sweet wines as other people are about dry and I rarely drink Ports. I'm the perfect person to sit next to when they start passing around the '55 Fonseca because I'll gladly give you my share.

I'm not fussy about glassware, except that I hate the way red wine looks in a Champagne flute.

WHY RED WINE?

Red or white? It's the first question you're asked when you are ordering wine in a restaurant or browsing in a wine store.

I chose red for this book because red wine is hip and sexy now. Everywhere I go, I meet more and more smart, beautiful young women who prefer red—even as an aperitif. This new generation also smokes cigars after dinner.

For many people, my husband included, red wine is real wine. And most people are said to follow a natural progression in wine drinking, graduating from sweet to white to red.

Red wine is more complex than other wines. That's considered its chief virtue. There's just more going on in a glass of red wine than with white. One could even argue that the same measure of complexity would be a flaw in white wine.

Historically, red wine was practically the only commercial wine—other than sweet wine or fortified wine, such as Sherry. Without very modern chemistry, dry white wine oxidizes very quickly, whereas red wine contains natural preservatives, which come from the skins. Until the late '50s, most dry white wines were always best drunk locally. Only now are white Bordeaux coming into their own to the extent of getting much beyond the château walls.

An additional and very large part of red wine's attraction is all of its positive health benefits. Demand started increasing when Morley Safer made the "French paradox" famous on *60 Minutes.* When my grandaunt, an inveterate martini lover, heard about it, all she wanted to know was *which* red wine. Then, for a while, there was some thought that the health benefits could be attributed to all wine or maybe even just alcohol, but the reigning wisdom among medical experts today is that there are certain other ingredients in red wine—again, in the skins—which make it the latest health drink.

What exactly is in the skins? Not all of the chemical compounds have been identified, which is why new health-related information keeps coming out, but the known components, or phenolics, include pigments, tannins, flavor, and a compound called resveratrol, which the scientists believe is the source of wine's cholesterol- and cancer-fighting benefits.

Certainly, red wine's most salient characteristic is the color. Red is said to excite the senses more than any other hue in the spectrum. It's life, death, passion, and love, as well as the best remedy for sadness. Perhaps part of red wine's appeal is that it *is* visually stimulating and thereby heightens our sense of smell, which is so much a part of wine tasting.

Red wine is made entirely differently than white wine. It is fermented with the skins, whereas white wine is fermented juice only. All of the color of red wine comes from the skins. If you peel a Cabernet grape, Mae West style, and rub the skins between your fingers, the color of red wine will come off on your hands; the meat or heart of the grape is clear.

There are many shades of red. Young Cabernet is purple, Bordeaux is a color unto itself—though each of the First Growths casts a particular hue, Pinot Noir is ruby red, and Barolos turn from garnet to amber. Some varieties are more colorfast than others. Freshly crushed Petite Sirah is as indelible as beet juice, and generally, young wines stain worse than old ones.

Certain museums, the State Department, and Neiman Marcus department stores won't even allow red wines when they hold parties, for fear of ruining the rugs. And after the Northridge earthquake in 1994, a good friend of mine learned a very painful lesson about displaying prized red wines in a white-carpeted living room.

Probably the best piece of consumer advice I can give is how to remove red-wine stains. One way is to immediately cover the spot with salt to blot the color. Another is to drench it with white wine, or better yet, Champagne, and then rinse it out with hot water. A word to the wise is never wear white to a wine tasting unless you are feeling particularly invincible.

The great truth about wine is that you don't have to know anything to know what you like. It's very liberating to learn that even the experts disagree. Berkeley-based wine importer Kermit Lynch, in his book *Adventures along the Wine Route,* called Jean-Marie Peyraud, the winemaker at Domaine Tempier, his favorite tasting companion because they differ on almost everything. Conversely, part of the enjoyment of getting to know someone is discovering you have kindred palates.

The only way to develop opinions is to taste. My advice is to find a good wine merchant—Thomas Jefferson corresponded with his for years—and go to wine festivals and charity wine auctions. The advantage of these kinds of tastings is that you can usually meet at least one winemaker or someone from the winery, and with luck you'll become like a friend of mine in Atlanta who only drinks wines made by people he knows.

Here is another sage practice I learned from a traveling businessman. The first thing he does when he checks into a hotel is find out if there's a winemaker's dinner going on in town so that rather than eat alone, he'll sit down to a special menu with wines to match and, at the very least, meet like-minded people who enjoy food and wine.

When to drink a wine varies with the grape, the age of the vineyard, the vintage, and personal taste. Wines age on a bell curve. Determining the peak moment is like trying to gauge the momentum of a sunset and depends on whether you prefer to catch it on the upswing or the downswing. The producers all have their opinions of when their wines will be at their height, though each would admit to being wrong more than once. It is pure conjecture. Many lovely evenings can be spent over a bottle of wine discussing how long you think it will live—not merely hold up but evolve into something more interesting.

Then there's reality.

Most people drink very young wines today, having neither the space nor the inclination to store them while they age. The wineries release their reds two to three years after the harvest for cash flow and the distributors are eager to turn their inventories as well. Most of what you see on wine lists and on the retailers' shelves—even in Paris—are current vintages, which just a generation ago would have been considered simply too young to serve with a meal. The trend has pushed winemakers to produce more accessible wines, a style or innovation made feasible by modern winemaking technology.

This isn't the first time there has been a shift in taste from old to new. The ancient Greeks wrote about the pleasures of older wines, but in the seventeenth century, *vins de l'année* were more highly prized because they were more likely to be sound. In Thomas Jefferson's time, "good and old" was the order of the day, and now we're back again to drinking them young.

How a wine ages depends first on the grape and how each variety absorbs oxygen. Producers can see how much more slowly Cabernet Sauvignon absorbs oxygen in the barrel compared with Pinot Noir or Merlot.

Fruitiness and the strong presence of tannins are the two primary signs of youth in a wine, both of which weaken or mellow with time. Wines generally seem more tightly knit when they're young and become more expansive with age. The depth of flavor and richness may be hidden in a young wine like a tight rosebud, compared with the full-blown flower that they are in a more mature wine.

For a wine to age well, it needs the following ingredients: strong varietal character and structure—tannins, acidity, and alcohol—which help a wine open up with cohesion and grace. Tannins give the wine oomph. Acidity adds brightness and lengthens the finish. Alcohol adds body. The keystone is balance.

Wines with an alcohol content of 13 to 13.5 percent normally age longer than do wines with a content of only 11 percent. Wines with over 20 percent alcohol, such as Sherry, Madeira, and Port, can age for centuries and still be alive and sometimes quite delicious. Champagnes and Sparklings are the exception. They're lower in alcohol than big red wines, but during the time they're aging on the yeast before disgorging—before the cork is put in the bottle—they can live practically forever because hardly any oxygen gets into the wine.

Vintage counts. Some vintages are "lighter" than others—they don't have the weight or richness associated with longevity; or they're "thin," which can be reflective of rain in September; or they're so full flowered and fruity from a short, hot summer that they don't seem to have the staying power. Price is not necessarily a means of inferring a wine's longevity. A perfect example is 1982 Bordeaux, which, despite being a great year with prices to match, are nonetheless ready to drink, which is neither good nor bad, but it would be a pity to let them go over the hill.

The age of the vine is another factor in how wines age. The older the vineyard, the more long lived the wine. This was always the excuse for why California Cabernets perhaps did not age as well as Bordeaux and calls into question what the effects of replanting because of phylloxera will be in California for the next ten years. In the short term, phylloxera may slow down the work involved in building collectible wines.

Another factor is that consumer taste is running to very soft, young, instantly friendly wines. The new generation of wine drinkers has a different frame of reference than do their parents, who were weaned on French wine. Those who start with California wines will always have a taste for fruit in their wines. It's natural in the same way that the emotional response to certain smells is not universal but rather a matter of experience.

I think another determinant is the training of the winemakers. There aren't any secrets anymore. Ideas and technology are traded around the world. The best young Burgundy producers are far from insular and the finest California winemakers are not only informed by the great European traditions but also borrow from the Australian advance in viticulture.

All wines are different from what they were 15 years ago. First of all, they're better. You have to work very hard to find a bad wine today. They're generally more gently pressed, less extracted, less tannic, driven by consumer demand for fresher, brighter wines to go with the way we eat and live. And there are more wines. Every year is a vintage year somewhere in the world.

Technology makes the fashion for young wine possible. Winemakers can create wines that are soft and supple because the presses used are gentler than any previous method of extracting juice from the grape. By pressing lightly, we can avoid the harsh tannins that make a young wine seem gripping. We can keep the wines bright by avoiding oxidation and the wild bacteria that grow over time when the wine is in the barrel.

Or we can give new releases a kind of instant patina so they will have some of the characteristics of aged wine. These techniques include extended wood aging. A woody flavor in wine can give most people the impression of maturity, as does reducing the acidity, which makes the wine seem more opulent and has the effect of accelerating the aging process. The processes of achieving instant patina are neither better nor worse than more traditional winemaking methods. They're just part of a different philosophy. My sense is that winegrowers naturally place more emphasis on the fruit in their wines, while winemakers who buy grapes may want to show more technique.

There is the risk of losing some individuality and falling into an international style, but what's so fascinating is that you can go from winery to winery and hear completely different opinions on how wine should be made. Winemaking is a series of a thousand interlocking and compounding visceral decisions. Each winemaker is adamant that he or she knows the best way to go about it. In that sense, they are like novelists—individual voices, each telling a story. There are so many interesting variables—the grapes, the vintage, the ebb and flow of creative energy. The one unifying factor is that every vintner I know makes wines that are meant to be enjoyed.

VINEYARDS, WINERIES, AND WINEMAKERS

In an ideal world, all wines would be organized by vineyard. The vineyard is everything—soil, climate, lay of the land, exposure to the sun, all of which add up to whatever distinctive qualities you can find in a wine. The French talk about *terroir.* I would say that the closest translation for *terroir* into English would be "vineyard" because the vineyard holds a special magic: the ability to be unique.

It takes years of practical experience, mapping out the vineyards, to determine which grapes go where and, beyond that, where they grow best. The goal is to produce a wine distinctive enough to be identified by the vineyard over the variety, capturing the quality of the vineyard and honing in on its distinguishing characteristics—some identifiable smell and taste that you pull out of the ground to create a wine that people ask for and seek out. The French have been working at this for centuries, whereas we Californians have successfully jumped over several generations, telescoping 100 years into about 25.

It is much easier to pick a wine by vineyard in France than it is here. The Bordeaux tradition is to make one wine, not counting an obscure white or lesser-quality second label. Few consumers know or really care about the varietal composition. In Burgundy, the grape is a given. Most California vintners, on the other hand, plant a wide range of grape varieties and make several different wines.

I rank Beringer Vineyards as the best all-round winery in California for their expensive, highly rated Private Reserve to their equally acclaimed Napa Ridge at the exact other end of the price spectrum. They own 10,000 acres of grapes, acquiring much of it in the last eight years along the central coast. Winemaker Ed Sbragia has been with Beringer since 1976. Vineyard manager Robert Steinhauer is considered one of the best in the business. This is a winery known for not cutting any corners. Their red-wine program centers on great vineyards in Knight's Valley, Bancroft Ranch on Howell Mountain, and Chabot on the eastern slope of Napa Valley.

E & J Gallo Winery is by far the largest in terms of volume, producing 60 million cases a year. I can't even imagine that many bottles, but I am fascinated by Gallo. The story goes that Ernest Gallo, the marketer, claimed he could sell all the wine Julio could make, and Julio answered that he could make all the wine his brother could sell. Today, you can walk into a California grocery store and see an entire aisle with floor stacks of Turning Leaf, Zabaco, Blossom Hill, Gossamer Bay, Ecco Domani, Indigo Hills, Marcelina, and Anapamu, all Gallo premium products. The Gallos are the largest landholders in Sonoma County and their luxury brand, E & J Gallo Sonoma Estate, is perennially sold out, fulfilling the brothers' dream of producing a first-class wine with their name on it. Gallo of Sonoma also focuses on individual vineyards in Dry Creek, Russian River, Alexander Valley, and the Sonoma Coast.

A number of winemakers, however, feel that region is more important than any one vineyard. Dick Arrowood, for example, who made his name as the fair-haired winemaker at Château St. Jean in the early '70s with vineyard-designated Chardonnays, feels very strongly that the best wines are the sum of many parts. He argues that variety—using grapes from a number of different vineyards from the various parts of Sonoma County—offers more possibilities, more elements to work with, and a better shot at greatness.

Kendall Jackson's most expensive bottlings, their Grand Reserves, bear a California appellation, which means the grapes can come from anywhere in the state. Their reputation depends entirely on the blend.

The style and fame of certain winemakers can supersede both vineyard and grape. These are the mandarins—winemakers who are brand names unto themselves. Among them are Heidi Peterson Barrett who makes Screaming Eagle, Grace Family Vineyards, Vineyard 29, and Hartwell; Gary Farrell, Paul Hobbs, Jed Steele, and Cathy Corison, who make their own eponymous labels; and Tony Soter of Araujo, Dalla Valle Vineyards, Etude (which is Tony's own label), Niebaum-Coppola Estate Winery, Spottswoode Winery, and Viader Vineyards.

Helen Turley is *the* consulting winemaker of the moment whose trademarks are concentration, softness, and rarity—big, dramatic wines, bursting at the seams with flavor. She won't touch a wine whose production exceeds 500 cases. Her reds include Colgin Cellars, 250 cases made from a Napa vineyard owned by Ann Colgin, a very sharp Texan who heads the rare-wine auction department for Sotheby's in Los Angeles, and Lewis Cellars, owned by Randy Lewis, a former race-car driver with a booming laugh.

Randall Grahm of Bonny Doon Vineyard can be relied on for all the offbeat varieties. He makes everything but Cabernet, Merlot, and Pinot Noir, tends his own vineyards in the Santa Cruz Mountains, but has no problem going farther afield to source grapes up and down the state.

Although all these factors—vineyard, history of the winery, and bent of the winemaker—are fascinating, the main point for you the reader, and for me, is what tastes good. So, here is my particular tilt on some of the choices available to you. I hope this book makes you very thirsty.

California Cabernet

◆◆◆◆◆◆◆

DECISIONS, DECISIONS

Cabernet Sauvignon is California's best red grape. It's what we're known for, it's the most widely planted, and it fetches the highest dollar. Cabernet is still king; I don't think Merlot or Zinfandel, though highly fashionable, are in any position to knock Cabernet off its pedestal just yet.

Reputations may nudge forward or drop back periodically, but there are at least 50—maybe even 100—genius, highly individualistic, opinionated California Cabernet producers, all vying to do the same thing—make great wine.

The one category that's difficult to fill is the $10 and under. For that, you have to turn to Chile, Australia, Italy, and southern France. Fifteen dollars will buy "pretty good" California Cabernet, which in the context of the history of wine is an exceedingly high standard. But you can walk into a wine store and, for $20 and over, see an entire wall of choices, which are not just good but *very* good to outstanding. The difference is that each of these will have something—some distinguishing characteristic, story, or personality—that makes it special.

Cabernet is a young grape compared with an ancient variety like Syrah, as it dates back to only the seventeenth century. The scientists, using DNA analysis, say it's a surprising, but lucky, natural cross between Cabernet Franc—a red-wine grape, and Sauvignon

Blanc, which is white. The eighteenth century was its heyday in Bordeaux—remember, Thomas Jefferson's favorite Château was Lafite, or "la Fite," as he spelled it. It remained dominant in Bordeaux until the end of the nineteenth century, when it was supplanted by Merlot because Merlot is less susceptible to shatter, a serious practical problem in a region prone to humidity and spring rain.

California became famous for its Cabernets in the 1890s. We were the up-and-coming wine-producing area of the world, as highly regarded internationally then as we are today. One of the most famous wineries of the time was La Questa, known especially for Cabernet Sauvignon, which naturally wowed the rest of the wine-drinking world with its gorgeous, vibrant, exuberant California fruit. Now, almost everyone in California makes at least one—if not two or three—different labels each year—counting special bottlings, reserve wines, and second labels, amounting to at least 1,000 different labels in the state.

It seems absurd to me to have to pick any one favorite. Why not try them all? I'm very fickle. My recommendations show a clear bias for a particular style, but my favorites today won't be my favorites next month.

Nonetheless, there's something macho about Cabernet that seems to bring out the competitive streak in most people, making them less concerned about nuance, as with, say, Pinot Noir, and more interested in just who's the best.

One standard is the now famous 1976 Paris tasting, which woke the whole world to California wine when a panel of distinguished French tasters, to their everlasting embarrassment, preferred 1973 Stag's Leap Wine Cellars over 1970 Château Mouton-Rothschild, forever dispelling the dogma of French superiority and showing rather publicly that even the most sophisticated palates can confuse Bordeaux and California in blind tastings.

Another hierarchy is set at the rare-wine auctions. The three dominant wines are Stag's Leap Wine Cellars, Caymus Vineyards Special Selection, and Heitz Martha's Vineyard. Only one Sonoma wine does well in this arena—Silver Oak Cellars' bottling from the Alexander Valley.

You can't talk about California Cabernet without acknowledging Mondavi. There's a tendency to think Mondavi has become too corporate to be good anymore. They now produce over 6 million cases of wine a year, most of which is made at their Woodbridge winery in Lodi. But the Mondavi and Mondavi Reserve Cabernets are Napa Valley classics and hold up very well with the times.

Jordan Vineyard & Winery staked its claim in the metamorphosis of California Cabernet as the progenitor of soft, pleasing, easy-to-drink reds. The philosophy behind this wine was to be as comfortable as an old sweater. This is one of the reasons why it dominated the market for so long. Now almost everyone is making wonderfully delicious Cabernet to drink the day it is purchased, though Jordan still has "the name."

In the realm of current releases, the most expensive are Caymus Special Selection at $135 a bottle, followed by Groth Reserve at $130, Stag's Leap Wine Cellars, Cask 23 at $120, Diamond Creek Vineyards, $100, and Opus One, $100.

Diamond Creek is perhaps the polar opposite of "my" style of Cabernet. I describe it as orthodox Napa-style Cabernet, which comes across as a clenched fist with biting tannins that taste like a green persimmon. The fascination of Diamond Creek is the intensity of fruit with all that tannin, which eventually yields a remarkable wine, albeit in the big, old-fashioned style—if you are willing to wait for perhaps 10 years. Most winemakers have taken the opposite track, trying to create Cabernets that are more approachable in their youth, but not proprietor Al Brounstein. And as much as his three distinct vineyards—Red Rock Terrace, Gravelly Meadows, and Volcanic Hill—show through in the wine, I think that part of what you're tasting in the wine is in fact his sheer willpower, represented in the tannins.

My pick of all the really famous names is Silver Oak Cellars—partially because it is owned by Justin Meyer, who was a Christian Brothers monk who had taken a vow of poverty and left the order with absolutely nothing to make his own wine, disproving the myth that wineries are all owned by people who earned their money doing something else.

A second distinguishing feature of Silver Oak Cabernet is that it is aged in 100 percent American oak. Justin feels that the value of French oak at twice the price of American is purely public relations. I happen to disagree. I think American oak imparts a strong, distinct, sweet flavor, but it's fascinating to hear an opposite view. Justin also makes a Napa Cabernet in the same luscious, full style but with a bit more earthiness.

I know the most about the Alexander Valley because that's where T-bar-T, Forrest's vineyard, is located. It lies one ridge over from Napa and is slightly cooler than Napa because it's on the ocean side of the mountains, catching a cool breeze off the Pacific, producing elegant wines with a distinctive bright fruit character—like blackberries, black cherries, and plums—not heavy, but vivacious and delicious for early drinking, with what we call soft tannins, which practically melt on your tongue.

The best Cabernet vineyards in the Alexander Valley dot the rocky, poor, well-drained benchlands in the northeast corner of the valley in the neighborhood of Geyser Peak Winery and Murphy-Goode. Kendall-Jackson Vineyards and Winery, Ferrari-Carano Vineyards & Winery, and E & J Gallo have recently planted hillside vineyards in this part of the valley. Jess Jackson bought the old Gauer Ranch, which my husband, Forrest, used to ride across when he was a kid. These vineyards are young but will produce great wines in the years to come.

Jordan Vineyard & Winery lies to the west, Alexander Valley Vineyards is on the eastern rim, and most of Simi Winery's holdings are in the south, on the cusp of Chalk Hill.

I have always had a strong feeling for Simi because of its history. It has a tradition of being run by women, from Mrs. Haig, who held on during the tough times of the 1940s and '50s, to Zelma Long, considered a winemaker's winemaker because of all the experimentation especially in the vineyards, which she spearheaded in the 1980s. Now the winemaking is evolving under winemaker Nick Goldschmidt to become suppler and more focused.

I'm also very interested in Daryl Groom's wines at Geyser Peak Winery. I think they represent a new American style, driven by an Australian style of winemaking that brings out the most fruit, that will become more recognized in the future.

Christina Benz is doing an exceptional job of capturing the Alexander Valley for Murphy-Goode. Margaret Davenport makes consistently really good wine—and a lot of it—for Clos du Bois. Château Souverain is without doubt the best value of the area.

Sonoma Mountain, home to Laurel Glen Vineyards, produces wines with less fruit, more strength, and more tannins than the Alexander Valley, in part because the terrain is steep. But it is still characteristically

Sonoma—stylish and juicy—because the elevation keeps it relatively cool and because although the late-afternoon sun pounds on the western slopes, which might produce harsh, excessive wines, Laurel Glen's vineyards face east, thus enjoying a long, drawn-out dusk.

Winemaker Patrick Campbell is a Harvard graduate in the philosophy of religion who first came to Sonoma Mountain to join a Zen commune in the early '70s and has since built a business that produces 40,000 cases of wine a year with his second and third labels, Counterpoint and Terra Rosa. Terra Rosa is made from Napa grapes and some years from Chile's Valle Centrale when California crop levels are low. The idea of bringing in grapes from another country is deplorable to me, but Patrick makes some fantastic wines.

Carmenet, across the road on Moon Mountain, makes huge, very full wines. One of the characteristics of the region is a distinctive violet scent in the wines, which is particularly pronounced when the wines are young. And one of the nicest stories I know about the wine business involves Carmenet. It happened in 1996 when Carmenet lost forty acres of vineyard to a freak summer fire. The local wineries responded by giving them enough grapes to cover the vintage—in a year that was a short crop for everybody. The best part of the story is the quality of grapes they offered. I know this is a wine I will want to taste when it's released.

Sonoma Valley, which Jack London called the Valley of the Moon, is often confused with Sonoma County as a whole, but it is one of 13 recognized growing regions in the county. Here you find Arrowood Vineyards & Winery, comfortably nestled into a gently rising hillside.

Neighboring Kenwood Vineyards makes two outstanding Cabernets, Artist Series and Jack London, which come from a vineyard originally planted by the writer on the western side of the valley at the turn of the century. London's grandson replanted the vineyards in the '70s and Kenwood has had an exclusive on the property's grapes since 1976, making aptly tannic, heroic, brawny wines, packaged with a white wolf's head etched on the bottle. I feel Kenwood's best wine is its Zinfandel from this same vineyard.

The famous Monte Rosso vineyard also lies in Sonoma Valley. It was originally planted in 1850 and replanted after the first scourge of phylloxera in 1885. Louis M. Martini Jr., who emerged from Prohibition as one of the best winemakers in the state, bought the vineyard shortly after the Repeal. Now his son Michael is the winemaker.

Louis Martini's best current release is the Monte Rosso Cabernet. Monte Rosso also used to make a Barbera from this property. The vineyard is perhaps more famous for Ravenswood Zinfandel. And it was the backdrop for the movie *This Earth Is Mine,* staring Rock Hudson and Jean Simmons. Its innate and enduring value comes from its own quirky confluence of soil and climate—a combination of good drainage through shattered shale, which forces the main roots down, and southwest-facing exposure, so the vines get daylong sun, yet are cooled by being on the last ridge open to San Pablo Bay.

On the Napa side, cognoscenti no longer talk about "the Valley" as a whole. Specific regions have emerged. Increasingly, the most expensive, sought-after wines are distinguished by district, and even more specifically by vineyard.

Howell Mountain is associated with power and intensity. It gets the last rays of sunlight at the end of the day and sits above the fog line, yielding uncompromising, unreconstructed, heavyweight champions like

Randy Dunn's Cabernets—big and massive, like chunks of flavor, which need at least a decade for the tannins to soften. Dunn is one of Napa's mountain loners; he doesn't want to produce a drop more wine than he can physically craft and sell by himself. He was the winemaker at Caymus from 1975 to 1985.

Stag's Leap District, on the eastern rim of Napa Valley, is known for its supple wines and black current, plum, cherry, and raspberry flavors. This is obviously the birthplace of Stag's Leap Wine Cellars, whose Cask 23 represents a unique lot or batch of Cabernet, mostly from older vines. The rising star of the area is Shafer Hillside Select, which is the fruit of a two-generation father-son winemaking team.

Clos du Val Wine Co., Pine Ridge Winery, and Silverado Vineyards further define the district. Silverado is a Disney property, a prime piece of Cabernet real estate, magically perched over the Silverado trail, planted by Lillian Disney, Walt's widow, in 1969.

What I find fascinating is that none of these wines tastes alike; each has its own character, and yet there's a kinship that's hard to describe. The same words keep coming to mind—*blackberry, cherry, tobacco, chocolate, mint*—all the usual descriptors, but I swear to God, if you hold one up against the other, you can taste the difference.

Rutherford, on the valley floor, is famed for its "dust." The late André Tchelistcheff, California's legendary winemaster, coined the term *Rutherford dust* to convey a kind of earthy, dusty, faintly drying, but very appealing mouth feel that you can recognize immediately when you taste it. This region is exemplified most famously by Beaulieu Vineyards (which dates back to 1900), Staglin Family Vineyard, Freemark Abbey Winery's Cabernet Bosche, and also by up-and-coming Whitehall Lane Winery.

Beaulieu Vineyards produces Georges de Latour Private Reserve, one of the most particular and consistent wines made anywhere—unblended, purely defined Cabernet Sauvignon from designated vineyards. The first vintage of Georges de Latour Private Reserve was put into wood barrels in 1936. André Tchelistcheff started making that wine in '38. The 1951 vintage—a fabled vintage for California—is reputed to be one of Tchelistcheff's finest and is expected to hold for another decade. Tchelistcheff made the wine in American oak. The next generation began using increasing amounts of French oak in the '70s.

Nearby Staglin is based on 50 acres planted by Tchelistcheff in 1966, specifically with Georges de Latour in mind. And some say the Private Reserve is not the same now that those grapes are no longer part of the blend. I find their Tapestry to be a much better value. It has a thread of Beaulieu Vineyards Private Reserve, with that "dusty" quality, but brought up to the '90s. It's a wine I think André Tchelistcheff would be proud of.

I must tell you, as a kind of footnote, that many tasters believe that the famous "dust" is not confined to Rutherford wines but is a general mid-Napa Valley characteristic that is particularly hard to pinpoint because so much of the original Beaulieu Vineyards is owned by Andy Beckstoffer, a fabulously successful independent grape grower who sells to all the top names.

Oakville, located at the heart of Napa Valley, tends to produce giant, opaque purple Cabernets, such as those by Caymus Vineyards, Opus One, Mondavi Reserve, Far Niente Winery, Franciscan Oakville Estate, Groth Vineyards and Winery, and Swanson winery.

Groth Cabernet is actually a blend of Cabernet from Oakville and Merlot from Yountville to the south, which qualifies as an "estate" under the broader Napa appellation, but the Groths have planted Merlot in

Oakville in the hopes they will like it as much so they can eventually label their wine as all Oakville.

Swanson was founded by the family famous for frozen TV dinners. Its winemaker, Marco Cappelli, is one of the hottest around. Swanson is unusual for putting more focus on Merlot from this region than on Cabernet.

The famous Martha's Vineyard is in Oakville. The wine from this property is always associated with an unmistakable eucalyptus smell, which some think comes from the surrounding trees. There is often confusion that Martha must be Joe Heitz's wife, but Joe's wife is Alice. The vineyard was named after Martha May, the vineyard owner's wife, who with her husband Tom first started selling their grapes exclusively to Joe in 1966 and later became partners in the winery. The most sought-after vintages for collectors are 1968 and 1974. None were produced in 1993, '94, or '95 because of phylloxera. The first vintage from replanted vines was 1996.

One of the hottest Cabernets today, Araujo Estate Wines, is based on a specific vineyard, the Eisele Vineyard in Calistoga. The current vineyard was planted by Milton Eisele, a Kaiser Industries executive, and was made famous by one of California's first vineyard-designated Cabernets, made by Joseph Phelps Vineyards in 1975. Now Bart Araujo—a landscape architect and a developer from Santa Barbara—and wife Daphne have taken it to even greater heights.

Yet, even within a single vineyard, some blocks or sections are better than others. Screaming Eagle comes from a one-acre extremely rocky section of a 73-acre ranch owned by a real estate broker who specializes in vineyard sites. The rest of her grapes are sold to other wineries. The first vintage, 1992, was given away as gifts to friends and business associates. One bottle recently sold at a Christie's wine auction in Los Angeles for $700. And to show you how intertwined Napa's winemakers can be: Screaming Eagle's winemaker is Heidi Peterson Barrett, whose husband, Bo Barrett, is the owner/winemaker at Chateau Montelena and whose father, Dick Peterson, is best known for starting such large-scale operations as Monterey Vineyard and Atlas Peak Vineyards. Her sister, Holly, is a chef, married to Tim Mondavi.

Of the two "French contenders," Opus One and Dominus Estate, I root for Dominus. Opus is the joint venture between Mondavi and Château Mouton-Rothschild, has maintained a consistently high level of prestige, and now produces 30,000 cases a year. It began as a concept between two great men. It is a blend of grapes from several vineyards. There's a constant debate whether the result tastes French or Californian. The winery is a monument on Highway 29 that looks like an imperial white pediment or a launchpad.

Dominus Estate—owned by Christian Moueix, who makes Pétrus, one of the most expensive reds in the world—is a wine in evolution. It seems to be becoming softer. Production is about 6,000 cases. It is a step or so behind Opus One in price. Dominus is based on a vineyard—a special parcel called Napanook Vineyard, which its former owner, John Daniel, the epitome of Napa establishment, deemed to be the gem of all his holdings, including the original historic Inglenook Vineyards.

Dominus now has a new winemaker brought over from France, having just lost Dave Ramey, formerly of Matanzas Creek Winery, then Chalk Hill Estate Vineyards and Winery, who joined Moueix with the 1996 vintage and left in early '98. Dominus also has a new winery designed to meld into the landscape, which seems to reflect the more understated elegance of Pomerol, where Pétrus is rooted, compared with the imposing style of Mouton, Médoc, and by extension, Opus One.

Initially, Dominus was made at nearby Rombauer Vineyards, owned by the nephew of Irma Rombauer—she of *The Joy of Cooking* fame. He rents cellar space for fermenting, aging, and bottling to a number of disparate vintners, besides making his own wines.

There's a whole slew now of custom crush Cabernets, with labels I'd not heard of before, being made by well-known winemakers in rented space, often sourced from prestigious vineyards, produced in very small lots—200 to 500 cases each—and selling for about $30 a bottle. Custom crush wines are identified by the words *produced and cellared by*... on the label. One example is Cornerstone Cellars, which apparently I was the last to discover. Such wines can either disappear from the scene very quickly or skyrocket.

The Santa Cruz Mountains, where Ridge Monte Bello is located, south of San Francisco, is another place name to look for on the label. You can sometimes see them from the air, looping back over the water, on a bad-weather approach to San Francisco International Airport. The Santa Cruz Mountains look like a tight cluster of hills, all bunched together, jutting up from the ocean, covered in evergreens, with vineyards just at the very tops, and a thick block of fog off shore. The taste of this area is dense, earthy, and spicy with hints of black tobacco and cedar along with the fruit.

Mount Eden Vineyards and Cinnabar Vineyards and Winery sit on these hills. Kathryn Kennedy Winery, which has an incredible cult following, is situated lower downslope, on the inland side of the Santa Cruz Mountains. Her production is very tiny and the wines are very distinctive—an "old California" style intended for long aging. The vineyard is planted 100 percent Cabernet Sauvignon, all on its own roots, a highly unusual and risky decision because of the threat of disease and phylloxera.

I am fascinated by the emergence of soft, silky Cabernets from Monterey County, especially Carmel Valley, a mountainous area tucked between the Salinas Valley and the ocean, where a handful of growers and winemakers have made giant strides in how they handle their fruit. My favorite from this region is Marinus, a Cabernet-Merlot blend from Bernardus, owned by a Dutch entrepreneur who has a vacation home in Carmel. I love the softness and warm, ripe sweetness of fruit in their wine.

Washington State has also entered the picture. The majority of Washington's wineries are situated in the Columbia Valley, east of the Cascade Mountains, covering practically the whole southern half of the state—arid country, where agriculture is viable only because of water from the Columbia River.

Columbia Crest, its sister winery Chateau Ste. Michelle, and The Hogue Cellars are really the heart of the Washington wine industry. Their production levels are well over 1 million cases a year and cover every conceivable style. The quality is excellent across the board, and the wines all represent good value. I'll never forget that Forrest and I drank Columbia Crest on our honeymoon in Wyoming.

Red Mountain and Canoe Ridge are the hot areas of the moment for Washington reds. Hedges Cellars is showing the potential of the Red Mountain area in Yakima Valley, and California's Chalone Group, which owns Chalone Vineyard, Acacia, Edna Valley Vineyard, Carmenet, and Jade Mountain, is involved in Canoe Ridge, on the north bank of the Columbia. According to folklore, Canoe Ridge was named by Lewis and Clark because it looked to them like a giant, upside-down canoe almost a thousand feet in the air. Canoe Ridge makes only a small amount of Cabernet, focusing instead on Merlot.

Generally, I feel Washington State's Merlots are more exciting than their Cabernets, but the best names seem to be the same for both. Without doubt, the most

*Personal Recommendations**

EXPENSIVE

Bernardus, Marinus (Carmel Valley)
Corison Wines (Napa Valley)
Cornerstone Cellars (Napa Valley)
Louis Martini Monte Rosso (Sonoma Valley)
Simi Reserve (Alexander Valley)
Spottswoode Winery (Napa Valley)
Whitehall Lane Winery (Napa Valley)

MODERATE

Beaulieu Vineyards Tapestry (Napa Valley)
Château St. Jean "Cinq Cepages" (Sonoma Valley)
Château Souverain (Alexander Valley)
Cinnabar (Santa Cruz)
Geyser Peak Winery, Alexander Reserve (Alexander Valley)
Murphy-Goode Reserve (Alexander Valley)
Pride Mountain Vineyards (Napa Valley)

INEXPENSIVE

Hess Collection Select (Napa Valley)
Napa Ridge—Beringer Vineyard's second label (Central Coast)
Rodney Strong Vineyards (Sonoma County)
Terra Rosa—Laurel Glen Vineyard's second label (Napa Valley/Chile)

*N.B. Blends are included.

famous is Leonetti Cellar, which is almost impossible to find except in a few great restaurants in Seattle. Also well known are Woodward Canyon Winery and Ecole 41. My favorites are DeLille and Quilcida Creek, both small producers.

COMPARISONS WITH BORDEAUX

It's so tempting to describe California Cabernet as more rich, more exuberant, and much more "forward" than Bordeaux because of a greater emphasis on fruit, but that would be acting as if there is only one defining style of California Cabernet. If anything, there is more diversity today than ever. On the issue of fruit versus no fruit, I think the winemakers are meeting in the middle: Bordeaux winemakers are emulating Californian vintners by expressing more fruit in their wines and more California winemakers are adopting restraint, balance, and structure as part of their style.

And despite our own rising prices, most of California's top Cabernets are, as a rule of thumb, half the price of Bordeaux First Growths. Their current releases started at $1,300 a case *en primeur*—as futures, offered in 1997, two years before delivery—and shot up an additional 50 percent in just six months. Robert Parker predicted they'd go up quickly because there were so many buyers in line, but his pronouncements also tend to be self-fulfilling—kind of like the Alan Greenspan effect on financial markets.

Some say the Bordeaux market is tied to and functions like the U.S. stock market, with prices soaring whenever the Wall Streeters rake in multimillion-dollar bonuses. Others contend that only speculators watching the wine auction page in the *Wine Spectator* bought into the '96 vintage to hold it for 5 or 10 years as an investment, with no intention of ever drinking the wine.

The most salient characteristic of Bordeaux as an investment is its predictability. Name the château and the vintage and any experienced collector will be able to tell you exactly how the wine tastes. Some experts warn against ever investing in Burgundy because Burgundies fluctuate so much and because—except for Domaine de la Romanée-Conti—the production levels are so small there isn't enough from any one producer to sustain a world market.

Many Medoc châteaux can produce 10,000 to 25,000 cases of great wine. A few California Cabernet producers can compete with those numbers—Beringer, Mondavi, Silver Oak, Opus One, Caymus, and Chateau Montelena—but most still produce but a few thousand or only a few hundred cases.

And there will always be the classification of 1855, which has only changed once, in 1973, when after 20 years of intense lobbying Baron Philippe de Rothschild managed to get Mouton-Rothschild elevated to a First Growth. Since then, there have been a few attempts at reclassification. Gordon Getty staged a major tasting in San Francisco but then backed off the claim that it was to test or reevaluate the rankings, and every year, French wine writer Michel Bettane compiles his own classification, which in 1997 downgraded Mouton back to a Second Classed Growth.

The original Bordeaux classification of 1855 was based not on taste but on reputation and sales. And even if you continue to evaluate Clarets by the same yardstick, the top wine would be Château Les Pins, a Pomerol, made from mostly Merlot, which sells for over $1,000 a bottle and didn't even register on the charts ten years ago.

One question is whether prices can continue to rise, or if the bubble will burst as it did in 1973. The bulls say there's no comparison with the situation that led to a crash in '73 because there was a huge glut of inventory back then, whereas today there is hardly any great Bordeaux to be had, and the Asian buyers for fine wine had yet to become as significant as they are now. The most avid buyers today are mainland Chinese, who only want the most expensive wines, though the custom in Shanghai, according to the *Wall Street Journal,* is to drink Château Lafite mixed with Coca-Cola or 7-Up, which to me seems more appropriate than having a cellar full of gorgeous wines that have become too dear to enjoy. Still, the curmudgeons warn that if prices spiral out of control, there won't be *any* buyers, which can only lead to collapse; that Japan's prolonged economic crisis will eventually affect Bordeaux; and that we should worry what would happen if all those "millionaires next door" we read about decide to sell their unopened cases of Pétrus. Would a glut suddenly appear? In the meantime, Bordeaux has opened the door for California. More and more traditional collectors are turning to California, largely because of price, but also because Mother Nature has given us so many great vintages in the 1990s, whereas Bordeaux has suffered some difficult years. In truth, the burst of growth of the late '90s was unforeseen. When it turns around, we'll be surprised again. My father says he has seen three booms and two busts in a 25-year span, so guess what's next. The only question is when.

The perception still lingers that Bordeaux ages longer than California Cabernet. True or not, it's hard to say, because many reds are drunk up so quickly these days.

Winemaking technology makes the concept of gentle, young Cabernets feasible. The Australians barrel-ferment their reds, a nontraditional technique to bring out more fruit. Another method for pushing Cabernet into becoming more flexible is as old as the hills—exposing it to more oxygen, either at the winemaking level in the barrel or by decanting it before serving. I even recommend drinking one bottle over a three-day period—just recork it after dinner—so you can taste the wine's evolution.

Phylloxera may be a factor in how California wines age. Phylloxera has claimed 26,000 acres in Napa and Sonoma since 1982, with an estimated 17,000 acres on vulnerable rootstock to go. Its effect on California winemaking—indeed, on the very taste of the wines—is just starting to show. Generally speaking, the wines from young vines are lighter bodied, less complex, and less ageworthy than the wines from mature vineyards. They might need to be taken out of the barrel earlier because they can't stand up to as much oak and they may be released onto the market even earlier than we're accustomed to. Yet over the long term, the newly planted vineyards will be of much higher quality because we know so much more about viticulture today—the spacing of the vines, trellising, and clonal selection, or improving a vine variety to match a particular soil or climate—than we did in the late '60s and early '70s, when most of the vineyards in Napa Valley and Sonoma County were developed.

Most California Cabernet Sauvignons of the '90s are very different from what you generally tasted from Napa and Sonoma even a decade earlier. They are generally more accessible, are more supple, and have more depth and better structure—real structure, as opposed to just tannins. Part of the change comes from blending and other refinements, like barrel fermentation, but even more important is how viticulture has improved, from choosing the best sites for Cabernet to allowing the grapes to fully ripen so that the tannins evolve naturally from hard and astringent to soft and mouth filling.

Vintage Chart

1982 One of our favorite vintages. It was much more successful in Sonoma than Napa. I'm not sure I would venture much older than this for most California Cabernets. Further back, 1970 and 1974 were great years; 1968 is considered *the* vintage of the '60s. And 1951 is legendary, though I haven't a clue how the wines are holding up.

1984 This was always a "sleeper" vintage for me because it was so overshadowed by all the hype surrounding 1985. It was a short, hot year, resulting in ripe, fleshy, opulent wines. Iron Horse's is ready to drink.

1985 The most highly touted vintage of the '80s, extolled for having extremely rich fruit, thanks to a radiant summer, but I was saddened to hear from one collector that Silver Oaks Cellars' '85 fades in the glass. I advise drinking now.

1986 This is acclaimed as one of Napa's finest. The year was most memorable for the Valentine's Day rains and flooding that closed the Golden Gate Bridge. A cool summer produced more delicate fruit. You can enjoy the wines now or continue to hold onto them.

1987 The epitome of a very cool, dry year and one of our favorites because of an extra depth of character in our wines. It is generally considered a better vintage for Sonoma than for Napa. This would be my choice to open in 2000.

1990 Another drought year. We had one heavy rainstorm Memorial Day weekend that naturally thinned the crop. A cool August delayed harvest, allowing the grapes more time on the vine, intensifying flavor and giving better balance. This is another one of Iron Horse's favorites and an auspicious beginning to a long string of excellent years. It was an equally fine vintage in France, Italy, and Spain, making it one of the rare vintages that can bear comparisons of Cabernets from around the world.

1991 This is a wonderful vintage. A cold summer prolonged the growing season, and then it turned hot in September and October, giving the grapes extra richness. The wines are more fruit forward than tannic.

1992 Neck and neck with '91 in terms of quality, officially ending a seven-year drought.

1994 An exceptional vintage across the board. An extremely long, cool growing season produced deep, rich wines with concentrated fruit and texture. Every wine you taste from this year is delicious. I hope everyone bought enough '94s when they were first released (in 1997) and saved some for the new millennium.

1995 A quirky year, as is '96, which produced some fine wines but without the overall consistency of '94.

1996 This vintage will be newly released in 1999. Untimely rain during flowering in May resulted in a painfully low set, and by harvest time, the crop turned out to be even smaller than anticipated, which is like being all dressed up with nowhere to go. It is an early drinking vintage, not highly nuanced, but big, fruity, powerful, and bold, like a Dodge Viper, which is fine because of the short crop—the third short vintage in a row. It'll be fun to just drink it all up.

1997 A very early harvest. The whole year ran three weeks ahead of "normal." Budbreak was three weeks early; we had blueberries in June instead of July and harvested Cabernet in September, which we usually start to pick in the first days of October. The 1997 vintage was an anomaly for being both high quality and bountiful, resulting in the highest yield in the history of California. These will be wines to drink after the turn of the millennium.

The few attempts at a classification of California wines have been rebuffed. Bill Jekel, whose Monterey County winery is now owned by Brown-Forman, the Kentucky-based whiskey company, used to talk about it, urging it as a way to help guide consumers. Other winery owners perhaps had hopes of being somehow grandfathered in. But experimentation and innovation seem to be so much a part of what makes California wine American, and I think all of us are acutely aware that we're only as good as our next vintage. There's no doubt that the degree of difficulty—which does count in the Olympics—of growing grapes in Bordeaux is much higher than it is in California. We rarely get rain in the summer; our dry climate means we aren't as susceptible to bugs; and our cool nights inhibit funguses and molds. Nonetheless, we see remarkable differences from one vintage to the next. The marine influences vary from year to year and we don't get the same amount of fog. We can have a delayed spring, a wet spring, a combination of a cool summer and a hot fall, or a hot summer and a wet fall, which all make the odds of repeating a vintage seem impossible.

WHEN TO DRINK

When to drink a wine depends as much on personal taste as it does the vintage. To me, part of the enjoyment of Cabernet is the smell of violets and lavender. These smells are most pronounced when the wine is very young—still in barrels. After about 10 years, it develops a kind of library smell of leather and old books. I have decided that I prefer older Cabernets—at least 10 years old, when they're soft and mellow but still have fruit—but at Mustard's in Napa Valley, they're serving the current vintage of Dunn Vineyards by the glass.

FOOD AND WINE PAIRINGS

California Cabernets are made for rich dishes—or perhaps it's the other way around, that rich dishes, such as braised lamb shanks, marbleized steak, pepper steak, old-fashioned prime rib, hearty stews, duck with olives, and venison with dried cherry sauce, are made for Cabernets. I like a lean, elegant, lighter style of Cabernet—more likely to come from Sonoma than Napa—or an older vintage with chicken—a really rich roast chicken with herbs Provençal, sage, or rosemary. Lamb with rosemary is like three-part harmony with California Cabernets.

Cabernets can also be matched with everyday dishes, such as hamburgers and pastas with tomato sauce or pesto.

They are delicious with most cheeses, but not all. They can overpower fresh, young goat cheese. In my opinion, the single best cheese with Cabernet is Pecorino Romano.

And one way to prolong the time spent with a bottle of Cabernet at table is to serve dark, bittersweet chocolate for dessert. Chocolate and Cabernet will give you the sensation of a chocolate-covered cherry.

California and Oregon Pinot Noir

THE GRAPE

In an informal survey of 10 professional wine people around a luncheon table, five or six would want Pinot Noir if stranded on a secluded island, not only because of its versatility with food but mainly because of its potential for sensual indulgence, primarily in texture, what we call mouth feel. Yes, Pinot Noir is a grape with sex appeal—to both men and women.

There's a fine, time-honored tradition of talking about Burgundies in sexual terms. Colette, who wrote about sex better than anyone else has, won a wine writer's prize for an essay on falling victim to Burgundy . . . "his Very Willing Victim." The old guard still divides Pinots into masculine and feminine styles, but ask a Pinot Noir lover which one he or she finds the most virile or voluptuous and you're likely to learn more about the person than the wine.

Everyone knows by now that Pinot Noir is the most difficult, demanding, inconsistent grape to grow and the most challenging wine to produce. Forrest calls it Sisyphean because the moment you think you have achieved something special with Pinot Noir, the rock rolls back down, crushing you in its path. But he never gives up.

I've also heard Pinot Noir compared to golf in the sense that you never master it. It keeps you modest. Finesse often outdoes brute strength. And all the frustration makes any amount of success taste that much sweeter. But why? What makes it so captivating? I have a recurring thought that there is some kind of analogy with Princess Diana: The wine and the woman will always seem faultless in spite of—or perhaps even because of—their obvious faults. Part of it has to do with the physical aspect of the grape, which is thin skinned and vulnerable. Plus, it is incredibly variable. A vintage you didn't think much of at harvest, especially a lighter vintage, can—in the barrel or even later on, in the bottle—suddenly turn around and become delectable. This simply doesn't happen with Cabernet, which is much sturdier and straightforward and ages in a linear fashion. Mainly, Pinot Noir is extremely site specific. It loves a cool climate. Every California grower will tell you his or her vineyard is cooler and foggier than anyone else's—you'd almost believe we never see the sun in California.

The most sought after Pinots come from a handful of very specific zones: the Anderson Valley in Mendocino; Sonoma's Russian River and Green Valley, where Hartford Court, Iron Horse, and Marimar Torres Estate are located, halfway between a bend in the river and the Pacific; the Sonoma Coast; Carneros, which bridges Napa and Sonoma; the Central Coast, primarily Santa Barbara, which teeters on the edge between northern and southern California; and the Willamette Valley in Oregon.

Mendocino is a long drive north from San Francisco. There is no easy way to get there. It's very remote and therefore very pastoral. Jed Steele makes my favorite Mendocino Pinot Noirs. He's a big man, tall and built like a bear, but he has a very gentle nature, which comes through in his wines. Another Mendocino standout is Greenwood Ridge Vineyards. I recently tasted their 1995, which was very delicious.

I am partial to Pinot Noirs from the lower Russian River, a very delimited area that starts at the Rochioli Vineyard & Winery on Westside Road, encompasses the Joseph Swan and Martinelli Vineyards on River Road and DeLoach Vineyards on Olivet Lane, then Dehlinger Winery and Iron Horse on either side of Highway 116, winding up a bit further southwest at Marimar Torres.

The most important aspect of the region is the climate, naturally cooler, foggier, and more protected by hills than anywhere else.

We have an unusual, fine, sandy soil type, called Gold Ridge, which runs in ribbons through the vineyards, with fractured shale underneath for drainage. Exactly how Gold Ridge soil contributes to the taste of our Pinots is unknown, but it is definitely part of our belief system for why our wines have a particular berry flavor—kind of a cross between black raspberries and very mature strawberries—with a certain delicacy or refinement, spiciness, zing, and vibrancy that makes them easy and complex at the same time. Our breakthrough vintage was 1994, which I think had as much to do with the weather as with the will to succeed with Pinot Noir in this particular region, but we suffered from having very little wine to sell.

Carneros is also becoming more delineated. Francis Mahoney, owner of Carneros Creek Winery, and Rene di Rossa, who planted the famous Winery Lake Vineyard, are credited with discovering Carneros for Pinot Noir, but Mahoney has said that it wasn't until there was a critical mass of wineries in the area—Acacia, Saintsbury, Robert Sinskey Vineyards, and others—that the region, with its dry, windblown, sheep-grazed hills, started to gain recognition for having a particular bright cherry, jammy character.

The Sonoma Coast is still being defined as more

growers figure out how to develop vineyards without readily accessible water and how to emotionally and financially cope with anticipated periodic crop losses due to extremely marginal weather conditions. For example, the Camp Meeting Ridge Vineyard on a rocky, windblown hill behind Fort Ross on the Sonoma Coast rarely yields barely two tons per acre for one of my current favorite, difficult to find Pinots from Flowers Winery, fast on its way to becoming a cult wine.

Santa Barbara is also still being developed. Here, the most famous names are two vineyards: the 600-acre Bien Nacido Vineyard in Santa Maria Valley and Sanford & Benedict Vineyard in Santa Ynez Valley. The Sanford & Benedict Vineyard is a remarkable piece of land created by a landslide 20 million years ago. It is primarily made up of residual soil, weathered "in place," as opposed to alluvial soils deposited by rivers or streams. What are important are the drainage and how churt, a hard, angular stone in the soil, forces the main roots down very deeply. The valleys run east and west in Santa Barbara, instead of north and south as in Napa and Sonoma, so the ocean influence and the incursions of fog are much more direct. The best vineyards are closest to the ocean, but now Richard Sanford has purchased several hundred acres in a particular valley that he believes will be the new cutting edge.

There is a distinct style to Central Coast Pinots. Even though the Central Coast climate is cool and foggy like Sonoma's, there is a sweetness and a weight to the wines that is all their own. It may well be their coming from a lower latitude—that is, closer to the equator than Sonoma or Napa—that affects the angle of the sun and the length of the days. This is still just on the edge with southern California. The temperature rises by a full degree with each mile heading inland. Grape growing stops at the mountains. At any rate, the style of Central Coast Pinots sets them apart. Winemakers like Jim Clendenen from Au Bon Climat have really captured that style.

The most traditional California Pinot Noirs are Hanzell Vineyards and Joseph Swan Vineyards—big, rich, gutsy wines, which means lots of alcohol, full bodied, not particularly fruity, with lots of extract, as deep in color as Pinot Noir is going to be.

Hanzell was founded by James Zellerbach, a San Franciscan, heir to a great paper mill fortune, ambassador to Italy, and a dreamer. He was the first to question why we weren't making Pinot Noir like Burgundy in California. He copied a Burgundian *chai* (wine storehouse) from top to bottom, bringing the first French Burgundy barrels made from Limousin oak to California. This was visionary in 1959.

Joe Swan, an airline pilot with a passion for wine, came along about 10 years later. His winery was a 30′ × 40′ metal building. To put this in perspective, Forrest was working at the time for Rodney Strong at Sonoma Vineyards with 2,500-gallon stainless steel tanks—this was the prevailing concept of making Pinot Noir in those days—whereas the largest thing Joe had in his cellar was a 60-gallon French oak barrel. He did everything by hand. It was kind of strange; he would literally get off his jet plane and hand-siphon wine from barrel to barrel. His bottlings from the '70s are said to still be holding up.

I think of Chalone for Chardonnay, but their Pinot Noir is established as a very distinctive style—earthy, almost muddy, and traditionally need a long time to mature.

Chalone is not just a name, it's a place—wild, rugged, and secluded. It's formerly the home of a tribe of Native Americans, south of San Francisco in Monterey County, where, at 1,600 feet, temperatures can vary up to 60 degrees in one day. In summer months, the temperature ranges from 40 degrees at night to 100 degrees at midday, and there is as little as seven inches of rainfall in a calendar year.

David Bruce, a Santa Cruz doctor who has been gaining recognition as one of the most skillful and intelligent wine craftsmen in the state, makes a "Chalone" Pinot Noir.

Chalone is also a conglomerate of wineries, Chalone Group—Chalone Vineyards, Acacia, Edna Valley Vineyard, Carmenet, Jade Mountain, and Canoe Ridge Vineyard in Washington—that has a partnership with Château Lafite-Rothschild with interests in South America and was one of the first wineries to go public.

Acacia, before it belonged to Chalone Inc., was *the* Pinot Noir of the '80s. It was noted for being spicy and peppery, with more structure and lively acidity than the traditional style, and now it seems to be enjoying a kind of renaissance. Acacia belongs to the new school, which includes Iron Horse, Rochioli, Sinskey, Saintsbury, Steele, Tony Soter's Etude, and Jim Clendenen's Au Bon Climat. The unifying theme of this generation of wines is more intense, vibrant fruit, though Saintsbury broke out of the pack with a 1996 single-vineyard, 350-case-production Pinot that goes for $75 a bottle.

There's a certain very knowledgeable clique that seeks out Pinots made by Calera Wine Company, owned by Josh Jensen, a tall, lanky Yalie. In the '70s, he took off on a quest in Burgundy, worked crush at Domaine de la Romanée-Conti and Domaine Dujac, and came back with the conviction that truly great Pinot comes from limestone soils, rare in California. He finally found them high in the hills of San Benito, a strange, isolated, unique pocket 70 miles south of San Francisco. His winery is designed to operate solely on gravity, giving the must (grape juice, stems, and skins) the most delicate treatment imaginable. For many, he is Mr. Pinot Noir. His single-vineyard estate wines have a particularly strong following. They are named Jensen, Reed, and Selleck for three elderly gentlemen—Josh's father, Steve Jensen; Bill Reed of Seattle; and George Selleck of San Francisco—who encouraged and helped him pursue his dream. His "coastal" Pinot Noir, made from purchased grapes, is also very successful because it's affordable. Josh strikes me as a very quiet, sensitive, and private person, though he dresses like Elton John—bright red shoes, splashy shirts, crazy ties, and crazy socks—so it stands to reason that his wines are flamboyant and off-center.

You should be suitably impressed if served El Molino Pinot Noir, made by a very small Napa Valley producer. Many of the Sparkling Wine houses—"J," Domaine Carneros, Gloria Ferrer—are making limited quantities of still-wine (table wine) Pinot. And Warren Dutton, who has always been one of the top growers, is now bottling his own wine under the label Sebastopol Vineyards.

But the "gotta have it" Pinot Noir of the '90s is Williams Selyem. It depends on where you are on their personal mailing list if you can buy even one bottle a year. Most retailers come by it only when a customer of theirs trades in a bottle for two or three of something else, though sometimes hard-to-get wines turn up in the strangest places. You can almost always find a stash of Williams Selyem at the Brown Jug in Anchorage, Alaska, because Burt Williams goes fishing up there.

We first met Burt Williams and Ed Selyem when Ed was working as the wine buyer at Speers Market in nearby Forestville, where we shop. They bought some of their first Pinot Noir from us, which Forrest remembers being so high in pH that he was worried it wouldn't be good, but they made great wine from those grapes. The winery at the time was a rented garage, where they continued to make wine until the neighbors complained. Their current location is a corrugated metal building with a dinky salesroom and a plug-in radio blaring away. But I've heard that it's the one California Pinot Noir that's traded in Burgundy.

Williams Selyem was sold in 1998—no vineyards, no winery to speak of, just two years' worth of inventory and enormous goodwill—for $9 million dollars. Joe Montana was a prospective buyer, but he lost out to a New Yorker who owns Millbrook Vineyards and Winery on the Hudson River, a vineyard in Tuscany, and several hundred acres on the Central Coast.

Oregon is another world. McMinville, a small, not particularly scenic lumber town, has made itself the center of the state with an annual international Pinot Noir festival held in July at which you can show your wines by invitation only. There are about 50 Oregon wineries today, compared to about 900 in the state of California.

Beaux Frères, made by Robert Parker's brother-in-law in Oregon, is extremely highly rated. I tasted the 1991 vintage in the spring of '97. This was their first release and I was very interested in finding out if it would give me an insight into how Parker rates other wines. Beaux Frères is big, concentrated, made with indigenous yeast, unfined (unclarified), and unfiltered—all things Parker loves.

Using indigenous or wild yeast means allowing the natural yeast that is found on the skins of all grapes to do the fermenting. European-style native yeast fermentation is a controversial trend among Pinot Noir producers versus inoculating fermentations with clean, efficient, reliable yeast strains. The one problem with wild fermentation is that some of the yeasts are not viable when the alcohol rises over 10 percent. However, many believe that because the fermentation tends to take longer, the resulting wine has a more intense character.

Fining involves simply adding egg whites, gelatin, whole milk, or bentonite—a natural clay commonly found in Wyoming—to either settle out sediments in the wine or remove harshness or off flavors from the wine. Those who do not believe in fining say that using any of these substances pulls out flavor.

Unfiltered is a buzzword for Pinot Noir lovers. It means that the wine is more "natural," which can be good or bad. Unfiltered wines are likely to have some sediment in the bottle even when young, and they seem hazy. Some wines just fall brilliantly clear from the barrel, which is the ideal, but other equally fine wines can be lightly filtered to polish the wine without sacrificing character.

I think Oregon Pinot Noirs can be very good, but I don't think they're the best. Many of them taste more meaty, smoky, almost "bacony" to me. It's almost as though I want them to taste like our wines—to have the same fruit qualities—but they just don't. The Oregonians claim to have the cooler, more Burgundian climate, but we Californians find their summers too hot, and Oregon is prone to rain in September during harvest, which has led many to conclude that Oregon is more akin to Burgundy than California in having such erratic weather. Oregon is also allowed to chaptalize, which means to add sugar to the juice in a weak vintage to increase the alcohol and thereby the body of the wine, a process that is illegal in California. This is common practice in France, where it is called *soleil dans un sac,* meaning "sun in a bag." That said, the Burgundians I have spoken with tend to rate Oregon more highly than California, probably because Oregon's fruit tastes more like their own. Joseph Drouhin, one of the most famous of the Burgundy houses, was obviously making a statement about *terroir* when he settled on the Dundee Hills, southwest of Portland, to plant grapes at Domaine Drouhin. There's also a general perception in France that California wines are overoaked.

You should definitely drink Oregon Pinot Noirs when you're in Portland. One reason is that you can actually find them there. I would try St. Innocent Winery, Archery Summit, and Beaux Frères, which rarely leave the state. I like Brick House Vineyards, founded by a former CBS newsman whose intention was to start small and stay small; Paul Thomas Winery, which is also a very small producer; and Sokol Blosser Winery. Domaine Drouhin makes my favorite Oregon Pinot Noirs; the winemaker is Robert Drouhin's daughter Veronique. Her wines tend to be elegant, silky, and full of luscious, spicy, wild berry fruit, which reminds me of Russian River Pinots.

Recently, I had the opportunity to attend an exclusive tasting of some of Oregon's best from both the '94 and '95 vintages for the staff of the Sony Club on the thirty-first floor of the Sony Building on Madison Avenue with unbelievable views of New York and a marble staircase that is sheer fantasy. The production of many of these wines was literally two or three barrels (a barrel amounts to about 20 cases).

The 1994 vintage is perhaps Oregon's most raved about vintage since 1985 when the state first started capturing the limelight for U.S. Pinot Noir. The standouts were Domaine Drouhin's Laurene (named for the winemaker's daughter), which, after a shy first impression, opened up to a very rich, elegant midpalate with great fruit and a long, long finish; the Paul Thomas, which had an intense, spicy blueberry bouquet, brimming with youth, a supple midpalate, and a very long finish, and should be even more delicious in 10 years;

and Cristom Vineyard's Marjorie with its elegant fruit, youthful tightness, and very long finish. Cristom is a relative newcomer to Oregon. The winemaker is Steve Doerner, formerly of Calera Wine Company. The current wines are being made from purchased grapes while the winery's own vineyards are being developed.

Most of the producers I know feel '94 is atypical and overly tannic and prefer '95 even though it was a difficult year. They are not the blockbusters of '94 that have dominated the press, but many are elegant, complex, and delicious.

The delicacy of the '95 vintage was best represented by Ponzi Vineyard's very complex 25th Anniversary Reserve which had a very tasty core of spiciness. Ponzi is one of only two or three who can claim that much history in Oregon. The '95 Beaux Frères was meaty with full fruit and a lovely floral scent. Interestingly, the wood was relatively subdued in a wine known for its barrel character. Two other wines of note were St. Innocent's Freedom Hill and the Cristom's Mount Jefferson. Although somewhat restrained at the tasting, the '95 Adelsheim Vineyard showed great promise for the future. David Adelsheim was also one of the pioneers.

King Estate is the most widely distributed Pinot from Oregon. It's the largest, but the scuttlebutt is that the artisan Willamette Valley wineries shun King Estate for being from another region. King also represents the beginning of a new era in Oregon that has always been dominated by very small artisan producers with minimal capital and lots of heart. With the advent of King, Domaine Drouhin, and now Archery Summit—whose debut vintage was just 1994—we are seeing much more highly financed operations capable of building state-of-the-art facilities and buying all

Personal Recommendations

EXPENSIVE

Gary Farrell (Russian River)
Hartford Court (Sonoma Valley)
Williams Selyem (Russian River and Sonoma Coast)

MODERATE

Acacia (Carneros)
Byron Vineyard (Santa Barbara)
Dehlinger (Russian River)
Greenwood Ridge Vineyard (Anderson Valley)
La Crema (Sonoma County)
J. Rochioli Vineyard (Russian River)
Saintsbury Reserve (Carneros)
Sanford Winery (Santa Barbara)
Sinskey (Carneros)

INEXPENSIVE

Napa Ridge (Central Coast)
Saintsbury Garnet (Carneros)

the best barrels. It will be interesting to see if these wineries foretell a change in focus and style for Oregon. My gut reaction is that they will and that we may see more consistency from the region, which may also lead to fewer comparisons to Burgundy and more to California.

COMPARISONS WITH BURGUNDY

Not so long ago, practically everyone in the world believed that Burgundy alone could produce great

Pinot Noir because of the flavor and impressive individuality of each *cru* and *climat.* Many people perceive that French Burgundy is also earthier—has more of a *terroir* character, is more voluptuous—and ages longer but that only one in five red Burgundies lives up to expectations. Even a $60 bottle from a very reliable producer can taste just terrible.

They get wrecked in shipping because of the fragile, volatile nature of Pinot Noir. Poor storage also can be a problem, but mainly, Burgundies are cyclical. They go through unpredictable dumb or closed stages when you think the wine is dead, but in six months they come back in full sail. Collectors have always known that most Burgundies are going to be disappointing. They're a moving target. You have to catch them in a good phase to enjoy their true colors.

A more cynical view is that the growers select certain barrels for one market and send another bottling elsewhere. It's common practice for the best shippers, like Kermit Lynch, Becky Wasserman, Robert Kacher, and others, to each choose the particular barrels they want for their labels. In California, we make a master blend, which is distributed equally.

Burgundies also achieve a particular smell described in varying degrees as earthy to barnyard to funk, which can range from appealing to overwhelming. It can smell like autumn's initial decay, including a faint sweetness, like the scents of narcissus and lilac, for instance, which include alcohol indol, a product of decomposition, or it can have that familiar farm smell of manure drying in a field.

It's unclear if this character comes from the cellar or the vineyards. Some vintages are dense and intense and the same producer in another year will come out with a wine that's more up front and fruity. Nor is it apparent in all Burgundies. It seems to be more pronounced in older bottles and can be taken as a sign of a wine that's over the hill, suffered from bad storage, or was perhaps shipped in nonrefrigerated containers. It could also be a reflection of rot in the vineyard or plain bad winemaking. Dirty barrels can generate nasty bacterial problems.

California is said to be more fruit focused and dependable. If anything, our Pinots have been criticized for being too technically perfect and squeaky clean without character. And yet, as California winemakers get better at defining our regions, more similarities with Burgundy than differences seem to be emerging. Even our weather is getting worse. The last few vintages in California—1994 in Carneros, 1995 on the Central Coast, and 1996 in Sonoma—have been Burgundy-like experiences of producing next to nothing because of untimely rain either during flowering or during harvest.

Burgundy's vines are grown much closer to the ground—for warmth—than ours are. The tractors ride over the vines and the grapes are speckled cobalt blue with fungicide—mostly copper—to ward against bacteria, mildew, and rot. They use many more sprays than we do, and there is without doubt more mold and cobwebs in Burgundy's cellars than any other place on earth, but when you drink the wine, you just forget about it. They are also more tradition bound, which can be a double-edged sword. In Burgundy, a wine board still dictates the first day of harvest for every commune, before which nobody can pick a grape, a law we simply wouldn't tolerate.

But the most obvious difference between American Pinot Noir and Burgundy is price. I believe the reason the French command higher prices is simple supply and demand. There is a world market for Burgundy that

Vintage Chart

1985 Considered the breakthrough vintage for Oregon Pinot Noir. The growing season was hot and dry.

1986 Regarded as the vintage that brought Carneros into the limelight—a coolish year, a little shy on yield, but mainly because the weather and the area's winemaking skill came together in a collaborative effort to define and describe a regional style.

1987 The third in a string of excellent years in Sonoma. A warm summer led to a cool fall and a medium to late harvest. The result was ripe, berrylike fruit with body and structure. The wines are still aging well, best to drink in the next five years.

1988 At first, '88 and '89 seemed worth skipping. As lighter years, they have developed well with time and are now ready to drink. In particular, '88 Carneros Pinot Noirs are underrated because of the overall impression as a poor vintage.

1990 An excellent vintage in Sonoma and Carneros. Ready to drink, if you can find any.

1992 More than good, particularly so for the Central Coast. Most wines are still holding well.

1993 A lighter year in Sonoma, but one in which many of the wines have good backbone and have aged well. The fruit seemed restrained at first but is now coming out. These wines are ready to drink now. This is a very good vintage in Oregon. A late bloom and a long, cool growing season produced elegant wines that will continue to age for at least five years.

1994 A great year for Pinot Noir in western Sonoma. An exceptionally long growing season yielded wines with an elegant natural balance that you could taste in the grapes when they were still on the vine and in the juice as it came out of the press. These wines are tightly knit with lots of fruit, structure, and acid and should be at their peak after the turn of the millennium. This is also a highly celebrated year in Oregon and a very good but short vintage on the Central Coast.

1995 An especially fine year for Sonoma Coast. Burt Williams believes his '95 is superior to '94. It is a somewhat lighter, faster-aging vintage for Russian River and sadly, a disaster for quantity on the Central Coast because of rain during flowering. In many ways, '95 is a more typical year for Oregon than '94 because the wines are generally more delicate and less tannic, and though it was a difficult year—spotty quality because of September rain—there are many fine exceptions worth seeking out.

1996 A small, but flashy vintage for western Sonoma. The '94 vintage received all the press, though we like '95 more than '94, and '96 best of the three. These are wines that have been showy from the outset. More than likely, they will be drunk up young. Who can resist? It was also a high-quality vintage in Carneros, with the season starting early and ending warm, though volume was shy—off by about 15 percent. It was both a superb growing season and bountiful vintage on the Central Coast, helping winemakers recoup their losses from '95 with very intense, luscious wines. And it was another challenging year for Oregon because of summer rain, which diluted flavors.

1997 This is the vintage generally available for sale at the turn of the millennium. It might seem strange that we will be drinking wines so young, but one of the recent changes in winemaking techniques has been to apply a white-wine philosophy to creating Pinot Noir. Because it has such a delicate flavor, we want to capture as much fruit in the bottle as possible, so the wine is bottled after only one year in barrel rather than the two years required for other reds. We Californians are unrestrained about touting the quality of our Pinot Noir in 1997. One of the wonderful aspects of a great as well as bountiful year is that finding the highlights of the vintage is far less difficult. Unfortunately, the vintage was a disheartening disaster for Oregon because of rain at harvest time. In October, Oregon growers were finally pulling in their fruit, at disappointing sugar levels. But undoubtedly, exceptions will emerge from the pack, as in 1995.

Americans have yet to cultivate. Burgundy's biggest market is Japan, where labels count for so much. The United States ranks somewhere around eighth. And the best French producers just don't make that much wine. Joseph Drouhin, one of the biggest, makes 30,000 cases in total, mostly La Forêt, their inexpensive line.

I expect most California Pinot Noir producers would admit to being driven by Burgundy, even though in truth, very few Burgundies achieve that ideal we call Burgundian.

WHEN TO DRINK

For consistency, I recommend drinking most California and Oregon Pinot Noirs within five years of the harvest. After that, they tend to start showing more of their quirks than their harmonies, which you may or may not find utterly fascinating. One exception is the Pinot Noirs of Calera Wine Company, which come into their own only after 10 years. For the most part, Pinots are truly lovely to drink in their youth. I think the current interest in the variety, particularly in restaurants, is due to the fact that they are so good while they're young. Having a massive '96 Cabernet from Napa is just going to overwhelm that beautiful paillard of veal topped with fresh morels, but a young '97 Pinot would be sublime.

FOOD AND WINE PAIRINGS

Pinot Noir's chief virtue as a food wine is its versatility. Pinot Noir can make everyone happy even if you're ordering steak, and your dinner partner is having sea bass or roast chicken.

Almost everywhere you go to eat in Sonoma, you will be served either lamb or salmon with Pinot Noir. One or the other could be our national dish. Pinot Noir is my favorite wine with mushrooms. Try it with a meaty Portobello mushroom burger. It is my red wine of choice for grilled quail, roast duck, and Thanksgiving turkey. And there's a smoky flavor inherent in the grape that goes with smoked meats.

Pinot Noir is delicious with beet salad, grilled leeks, onion pizza, old-fashioned baked onion soup, or onion confit. It works quite well with many Provençal dishes: brandade, olive tapenade, roasted garlic on crusty French bread, soupe au pistou, stuffed squash blossoms, summer squash, and ratatouille. It'll even go with grilled zucchini. Pinot Noir is a vegetarian-friendly wine.

The most unusual and surprising match I've ever tasted was foie gras and Pinot Noir.

Pinot Noir and Brie were made for each other, though soft, fatty, blue-veined, strong, or salty cheeses don't work.

A pear poached in Pinot Noir is a wonderful autumn dessert—and Pinot Noir is divine with chocolate.

Merlot, Merlot, Merlot

HIGH BROW, LOW BROW

Merlot fits all the criteria for what a wine should be today—it's red and it's easy. You can drink it young. You don't have to think about it very much. It's compatible with almost everything, and it's fine by itself as an aperitif.

This is no passing fad. Merlot is here to stay.

One obvious result is that the prices of California and Washington State Merlots are climbing. Merlots like Columbia Crest from Washington State, which used to be $8 or $9, are now $12 to $15.

The bulk of the international offerings is under $10 a bottle. Vineyard, producer, appellation, even country of origin are just not very important for many Merlot drinkers in this price range. And most of it is pretty damn good, which is more than you can say about a lot of equivalently priced Chardonnay and Cabernet. Merlot, grown in a variety of climates and locations, usually can make good wine almost all of the time, but little in this bracket comes from California because our grapes are so expensive.

Even with a California label, the grapes could come from another country. Representatives from Fetzer Vineyards, Robert Mondavi Winery, and Kendall Jackson Vineyards and Winery are running into themselves trying to buy supply. Some of it is being purchased in bulk—direct from vats—in South America or Europe to be bottled in California and packed in gorgeous wooden cases branded with nothing but the word MERLOT in big letters.

At least a third of the Merlot being consumed in this country is imported. An entire flood of it comes from Chile, much of which may be, in fact, the rare Bordeaux variety Carmenère, and demand is such that the big wine companies, like Concha y Toro, are buying vineyards in Argentina just to fill the pipeline. The other major source is southern France, where the large cooperatives have hired Australian viticulturists to upgrade their warm-climate vineyards. Merlot favors a cooler climate and the Australians are expert at what they call "turning sunlight into wine."

There is plenty of Merlot in Italy. Most of it is light, slightly tart, everyday drinking wine traditionally from the Veneto, Friuli-Venezia Giulia, and Trentino-Alto Adige regions, as well as a handful of superb Merlots from Tuscany. Bulgaria has become another new supplier of lighter-style, high-volume Merlots that few Americans have tried. Bulgaria produces a vast amount of red, much of which ends up in the United Kingdom. Potentially, the quality could be very good with the advent of modern technology in the post-Soviet era.

Merlot is big business, and more new acreage of vineyards is being planted with it than any other grape. It has been the dominant grape in Bordeaux in terms of acreage since the 1930s, so in a sense, we in the rest of the wine world are just catching up, which is all to the consumer's advantage. This increase in supply should sensibly keep prices stable.

Merlot is traditionally a blending grape. Bottling it as a single varietal is an American phenomenon, which has spread internationally. Louis M. Martini Jr. is credited with being the first to release 100 percent Merlots in the early '70s. The taste is generally softer and rounder and has more strawberry-like fruit than Cabernet. It ages more quickly. The grapes ripen earlier on the vine, so it would follow that the whole natural process would proceed at a faster rate. How quickly it evolves also has to do with how this particular varietal sucks up oxygen, a difference from Cabernet that can be seen in the barrel. Merlot seems to me to have one clear note, whereas Cabernet is more like a chord of flavors.

This is not true for Château Pétrus—which is 95 percent Merlot, some of the other great Pomerols, and a few of the more extraordinary ones being produced in California, such as Beringer Vineyards, Howell Mountain, Duckhorn Vineyards, and Shafer Vineyards. An important note about these wines is that they are *not* 100 percent Merlot. They are blends with Cabernet Sauvignon, Cabernet Franc, or both, which gives the wines more backbone and structure. Despite the inherent softness of Merlot when mixed with the other Bordeaux varietals, these wines are really more enjoyable after some bottle aging.

Another distinction is price. There seems to be a rule of thumb with Merlots that the higher the price tag, the longer they can and should be aged, with the possible exception of Marilyn Merlot, made in Napa and released on Marilyn Monroe's birthday each June. This should be consumed within a year or two. Its collector status and appeal—bottles sometimes sell for $100—is more for the labels, and Marilyn Monroe's star power, than for the wine.

As of this writing, the most expensive California Merlot is the 1994 Journey from Matanzas Creek Winery at $155 a bottle. Only 2,200 bottles were produced. The wine sells out on release and has been dubbed the "Pétrus of California," though I prefer the regular Matanzas Creek Winery Merlot.

The best-selling examples of the soft, pillowy, easy-to-drink style are the Merlots from St. Francis Winery, Clos du Bois, and Markham Winery.

Serious or "high-brow" Merlots are moderately tannic, which might not be what you would expect, given Merlot's reputation for being ready to drink. And *terroir* does matter in this price range. Duckhorn Vineyards, for example, focuses on alluvial soil. Most of their vineyards are along creeks that go into the Napa River, so their soils are made up from sand outwashings, the rocks and gravel that water pulls down off the mountains and into the streams.

I am more enamored of Merlots from Carneros—such as Sinskey and Truchard Vineyards—which most people think of for Pinot Noir, but certain parts of this cool region—transition zones—really favor Merlot. The lion's share of the Merlot for Shafer Vineyard's bottling comes from their Red Shoulder ranch in Carneros. Pine Ridge Winery also sources Merlot from Carneros, and half of Matanzas Creek Winery's Merlot comes from Carneros. Generally speaking, cooler areas tend to produce wines that show more of the bright fruit of the variety, more herbal-spice, like fine dried herbs, and a bit more acid in the finish, which may aid them in long-term aging.

Forrest, my husband, has often said that Green Valley's cool climate might be perfect for a great long-lived Merlot. Iron Horse Vineyards doesn't need another variety, but the fruit that comes from a neighbor's vineyard next to our Thomas Road vineyard grows Merlot for Gary Farrell that is truly magnificent and may one day be vineyard designated.

Washington State Merlots tend to be more herbal because their climate is even cooler than California's. There are various styles, but Washington Merlots tend to be more robust and heavier than their California counterparts, which generally seem to me to be more

Personal Recommendations

EXPENSIVE

Duckhorn Vineyards (Napa Valley)
Ferrari-Carano Vineyards & Winery (Sonoma County)
Matanzas Creek Winery (Sonoma County)
St. Francis Winery Reserve Estate (Sonoma Valley)
Shafer Vineyards (Napa Valley)
Silverado Vineyards Limited Reserve (Napa Valley)
Swanson (Napa Valley)
Whitehall Lane Winery Leonardini Vineyard Reserve (Napa Valley)
Andrew Will (Washington State)

MODERATE

Benziger Winery and Vineyards (Sonoma Valley)
Beringer Vineyards Alluvium (Napa Valley)
Canoe Ridge (Washington State)
Columbia Crest Barrel Select (Washington State)
Columbia Winery Signature Series (Washington State)
Gallo Sonoma
Kunde Estate Winery (Sonoma Valley)
Pride (Napa Valley)
Sebastiani Vineyards (Sonoma Valley)
Sinskey (Carneros)
Truchard (Carneros)
Waterbrook (Washington State)

INEXPENSIVE

Blackstone Reserve (Napa Valley)
Estancia (Alexander Valley)
The Hogue Cellars (Washington State)
Hunter Ashby (Napa)
Louis M. Martini (California's North Coast)

delicate and refined. These wines remind me more of Bordeaux, which is not surprising, because they are on the same latitude, although the climates are very different.

Leonetti is considered the pinnacle of Washington State Merlots and is awesome. Andrew Will has a cult following. Columbia Milestone, Apex, vineyard-designated Merlots from Chateau Ste. Michelle, and Woodward Canyon Winery are also in the upper crust.

COMPARISONS WITH BORDEAUX

The best, most famous French Merlots come from Pomerol and St-Emilion, two of Bordeaux's eight provinces, located on the right bank of the Gironde, predominantly planted with Merlot and home to the most expensive red wine in the world, which is either Château Pétrus or Château Les Pins, depending on the vintage. Neither has a very long history: Pétrus became famous after World War II with the 1945 vintage; Les Pins' first release was 1981.

Pétrus comes from a small, 28.4-acre vineyard. The "château" is really an old farmhouse and the soil composition is unique—composed almost entirely of heavy clay rich in iron, compared to the prevalent mixture of gravel and sand or clay and sand all around it. Tiny, three-acre Les Pins, less than a mile away, consists of iron-enriched, gravelly soil.

Merlot is the dominant grape of Bordeaux, but to the best of my knowledge only one vineyard, Château Lafleur de Gay—a five-acre parcel belonging to Châteaux La Croix de Gay—is planted with 100 percent Merlot. Pétrus has 5 percent Cabernet Franc, though it doesn't always ripen enough to be included in the end result.

Certain Bordeaux vintages, like '85, seem to favor Merlot over the Cabernet-based wines just across the river. In other years, like '90, the advantage seems to go the other way. Apparently the same can happen in California, as in '83, which I remember as the "vintage from hell" for everything except Merlot.

In the 1990s, such producers as Christian Moueix, whose family owns Château Pétrus, began labeling their $8-a-bottle basic varietal wines by the grape name as a selling point, like we do in the United States, though there is an internal, oh-so-French struggle to make them delete the word *Merlot* and strictly follow the tradition of naming wines after their appellation.

WHEN TO DRINK

In most vintages, top-level California Merlots should be drunk four to six years after harvest. I prefer Washington State Merlots not more than two to three years old, probably because their vines are comparatively young. They suffered a tremendous setback in 1996 when a killer freeze in the spring wiped out 70 percent of that year's crop and, worse yet, forced many growers to hack back their vines to mere stumps or replant altogether. This has meant a four- or five-year wait for even a first crop and is interesting in the context of Château Pétrus, unique in Pomerol for having 70-year-old vines because the proprietress—Madame Loubat, whose niece now co-owns the property with the Moueix family—chose to wait the two or three years for potential recovery after a devastating frost in '56 rather than replant.

By comparison with Cabernet-based Bordeaux, even though some vintages can be held for decades, Pétrus is surprisingly quite enjoyable relatively young, though some collectors would argue that you should never drink Pétrus because it becomes so valuable with age. An unopened case of '61 most recently sold at Christie's for $50,000.

Vintage Chart

1983 Considered one of Washington State's greatest and an abject disaster in California for every grape except Merlot because of erratic weather. A heat wave dehydrated the grapes and then it rained during harvest, washing out flavors. One of Merlot's strengths is that it is less susceptible to shatter and, as happens in Bordeaux, there are years when Merlot tops Cabernet in quality.

1989 Great in Washington State and again difficult in California because of rain during harvest, though more growers were prepared for it this time.

1990 The first in an unprecedented string of very good to excellent years for California. The Duckhorns of Duckhorn Vineyards feel their '90 and '91 are coming into their prime, if you happen to have any.

1994 This was a great vintage in Napa and Sonoma and the top notch Merlots should be drinking beautifully in 2000. It was an equally fine year in Washington, where lower crop yields contributed to rich, concentrated wines. An aside: Italy produced some of its finest Merlots in '94, particularly Avignonesi and Castello di Ama from Tuscany and Bertanni from the Veneto.

1996 The '96s were released in 1998, but the best from California still need more time in the bottle. Like the Cabernet from the '96 vintage, they will show best in 2000. In Washington, the '96 vintage will be remembered for one of the state's classic winter hard freezes, which happen every five to seven years, and overall crop yields that were reduced by 50 percent.

1997 Hard to believe, but there are '97 Merlots available in '99. They are still young, but many are so showy you will want to drink them. Nothing wrong with that.

FOOD AND WINE PAIRINGS

Everyday, easy-drinking Merlot goes with Caesar salad, hamburgers, steaks, roast chicken, grilled fish, the deep chili flavors of Mexican food, and late-night scrambled eggs, though in my family, we believe the simpler the meal, the better the wine. I was just in a restaurant in New York that has 50 different kinds of melted-cheese sandwiches—a truly great place for drinking Merlot.

For fancier fare, Merlot and salmon with a Merlot reduction sauce or a cooked blueberry-and-wine sauce in the summer is a classic combination in the Pacific Northwest. Merlot with filet mignon is a steak house staple.

Merlot has a subtle bacon rind flavor to it, which goes beautifully with lamb, quail, duck, and venison and is fine with vegetables sautéed in butter or grilled with herbs. It can be served slightly chilled in the summer.

In general, complex Merlots are a flop with Asian cuisine. The dishes' fiery hot spices tend to overshadow Merlot or bring out the tannins.

A young Merlot is delicious with fresh goat cheese,

Asiago, a mild blue cheese such as Cambozola, and aged Gouda. An older one would be better with Morbier, Tomme de Savoie, and most semihard cheeses that hit the midintensity range. A really rich style, like Washington State's Leonetti, which for me is over the top in terms of fruit and new oak, *needs* cheese to bring out any snap and acidity in the wine.

Merlot does not work with chocolate the way Cabernet does. It doesn't go with anything with sugar, including salad dressings—sweetness is death to Merlot.

Zinfandel

◆◆◆◆◆◆◆

ALL-AMERICAN

Zinfandel fans seem to fit a certain mold—or have at least one heartstring that connects with big, gutsy, all-American, boisterous, unpretentious wines.

Zinfandel was widely planted in California during the Gold Rush, making it practically a native, as American and of the same era as Levi's jeans. During Prohibition it was the favored grape for home winemaking in basement cellars in San Francisco's North Beach. Its heritage includes strong ties to the Beat Generation. I imagine Lawrence Ferlinghetti drinking Zinfandel with Allen Ginsberg in the '50s. And then it became a Berkeley '60s kind of wine. It fell into disuse—except for white Zinfandel—in the '80s, to reflower as very much a wine for the '90s.

Part of its appeal is that you can drink it out of a tumbler—though there is a special Riedel glass for Zinfandel—and you don't have to dress up to appreciate it. We saw only one person in a coat and tie at the ZAP (Zinfandel Advocates & Producers) tasting in 1998. Most people wear jeans, and there's no makeup on the women, many looking very studious in their reading glasses—me included—in kind of a hip intellectual way, befitting the grape.

The ZAP tasting is the loosest, most laid-back wine event of the year. It takes place at the end of January in a great old warehouse on one of the long piers at Fort Mason in San Francisco, with the fog rolling right through the building and 100 or more winemakers lined up in alphabetical order along the walls, each behind a table, pouring samples of their interpretation of this one grape. There are several thousand tasters in a lovely mix of ages—more young people than we normally see at wine events—and there are many couples and a lot of women. There doesn't seem to be any spitting—the usual practice for professionals who want to avoid getting drunk—so that after an hour or so, it becomes a very relaxed and smiling group, with everyone's teeth purple from drinking so many young, deeply colored wines.

You can pick out the stars by the depth of the crowd in front of their tables. In 1998, you had to be very patient to taste Ridge Vineyards, Ravenswood, and Rosenblum Cellars Winery, who are called the "three Rs" of Zinfandel.

Ridge was one of the pioneers, seeking out old vineyards and keeping them separate as individual, handcrafted, distinctive small lots. In 35 years, Ridge has released over 300 Zinfandels under 60 different labels. Most are from very old vineyards that include Petite Syrah, Carignan, Alicante, and other obscure grape varieties used in traditional "field blends."

Joel Peterson of Ravenswood defines Zinfandel differently. His bottlings also come from great vineyards like Old Hill, Monte Rosso, Cooke, Belloni, and Dickerson, but they are 100 percent Zinfandel.

Kent Rosenblum is a relative newcomer. He is a large-animal veterinarian in "real life," with a winery in an industrial park in the East Bay across from San Francisco where he brings in grapes from all over the state to produce several small, vineyard-designated lots of handmade wine.

There were also big lines for Turley Wine Cellars, made by Larry Turley, and for Martinelli and J. Fritz

Cellars, where sister Helen Turley consults. Both of these wines have therefore become very difficult to obtain since Robert Parker crowned Helen the wine goddess. When I asked for other recommendations, a number of people said, "Well, Biale, of course." I'm embarrassed to confess I had never heard of Biale Vineyards before, though it was one of the standouts of the tasting, especially their Old Crane Ranch.

The biggest attractions were the "old vine" Zinfandels. Defining *old* for vineyards—whether it's anything over 30 or 45-plus—is as subjective with vineyards as it is with people. Is 50 old? Certainly vines 80 to 100 years old qualify. We have nothing like them for any other grape in California, making Zinfandel a unique taste experience with expressions of the same grape from so many great, old, and very distinct vineyards.

The old vines are our senior citizens. They stand alone; there's no trellising and they're head-pruned, so that the shoots come out of the crown. They are about three feet high and gnarled like an old person's hand. There are scarcely more than 1,000 acres over age 50 statewide, with the greatest concentration in Sonoma County and the Sierra Nevada foothills.

The yield from old vines is very low—nature's way of preserving a vine's waning energy—which has the effect of concentrating flavors. Perhaps age means that the root systems have reached a point where they suck more nutrients out of the soil while somehow adding another facet, more depth, additional nuance, extra complexity—though how deep the roots run depends on the soil.

Many winemakers think the viticulture style of the old vineyards may be as important as the age of the vines, so newly planted Zinfandel is being trained the old way. Although you could think that much of the allure of old-vine Zinfandel is simply romance, there is also an argument that a vineyard that wasn't pulled out or switched to another varietal after 100 years must have something special.

There is much delicious Zinfandel grown all over California. There are even 100-year-old Zinfandel vines in Oregon. And generally speaking, specific vineyards are more important than region. But the truest, the real essence—that optimally ripe, big, sweet, purple fruit—comes from Dry Creek in Sonoma County. A paradigm is made by Dave Rafanelli, who makes wines much the way his father did. Rafanelli Winery's wines sell for $16 to $17 in California. One of the pleasures of Zinfandel is that the best are moderately priced.

Dry Creek is a warm interior valley, which because of its proximity to the coast gets intrusions of fog that cool down the vineyards, prolonging the growing season. Even 100 years ago, the benches and hills with their distinct well-drained red volcanic soil were known to be best because they're not particularly fertile, which keeps the crop level low, an attribute that's important for Zinfandel because it tends to overproduce in rich soils, yielding lesser quality. For similar reasons, Zinfandel should not be irrigated, so it needs to be in a place that gets sufficient winter rain and have good drainage, which is why Dry Creek's hillside volcanic soils are so desirable. Volcanic soils let the roots run very deep, so the vines are drought resistant and can make it through harvest without irrigation. Dark soils retain heat, beneficial because Zinfandel is one of the last grapes to ripen. It needs to be fully developed—left as long as possible on the vine, not just ripe, but mature—or it can taste like cough syrup.

One problem with Zinfandel for the consumer is that there is a confusing abundance of styles with no indication on the label if it is going to be light and fruity akin to Beaujolais or restrained, Claret style, like

Personal Recommendations

EXPENSIVE

Chateau Potelle (Napa Valley)
Hartford Court (Sonoma County)

MODERATE

A. Rafanelli (Dry Creek Valley)
Bannister Winery (Dry Creek Valley)
DeLoach Vineyards—Single Vineyard (Russian River)
Fife Redhead Zin (Mendocino)
Gallo—Frei Ranch (Dry Creek Valley)
Limerick Lane Cellars (Russian River)
Pezzi-King Vineyards (Dry Creek Valley)
Quivira (Dry Creek Valley)
Rabbit Ridge Vineyards (Russian River)
Ravenswood's Monte Rosso (Sonoma Valley)
Ravenswood's Old Hill Ranch (Sonoma Valley)
Renwood (Amador County)
Ridge Vineyards' Geyserville (Sonoma)
Steele's DuPratt (Mendocino)

INEXPENSIVE

Cline (California)
Sausal Winery (Sonoma County)
Seghesio Winery (Sonoma County)

the Zinfandel by Clos du Val Wine Co. It can be big and rich like Rafanelli or fortified like Port. All of my recommendations are dry and have bright fruit. Fruit in wine is always my weakness.

Another issue is that there seems to be a trend back to bigger, more alcoholic Zinfandels, which some pro-

Vintage Chart

1987 Not a perfect vintage overall, but it was exceptional for Sonoma County's Dry Creek Valley. It's delicious to drink now if you have a taste for and a cache of older Dry Creek Zinfandels.

1990 The growing season was consistently hot, but not over the top, yielding opulent but well-balanced wines.

1991 A longer, cooler growing season gave wines with more elegance, definition, complexity, and exceptional acidity. The best will continue to develop through 2000.

1992 Another consistently warm year, with a generally big crop and soft wines.

1993 Another large crop and crazy El Niño weather made generalizations more difficult for this vintage.

1994 A storybook year. This is one I would choose to drink in 2000. Tremendous concentration but not overly intense fruit. Good acid makes these wines ageworthy.

1995 These wines seem more concentrated, bigger, hotter, not as approachable. Some say they will eclipse the '94s because of their intensity of fruit. They may not age well, but they should be stunning in 1999, if you can find any—the crop was very small.

1996 Another small crop. The young wines seem very good, but early on, they're not on the same quality level as the wines of the previous four years.

1997 One of the difficulties of the '97 vintage was keeping the crop levels small. The market is booming for Zinfandel and grape prices are at an all-time high, making it a great temptation not to thin the crop quite as severely as need be for the highest quality. Still, the vintage is being described as "epic," which to me says "high alcohol."

ducers feel is encouraged by the wine writers. But it may be the result of palate fatigue that the bigger wines stand out in comparative tastings. Or vintage may play a role, as the '97s, judging from recent tastings, have discernibly higher alcohol, which could be as much a factor of the year rather than simply a question of style.

WHEN TO DRINK

In general, I believe most Zinfandels should be drunk within six years of bottling to best retain their fruit essence. The best mature long after that. The trick is to catch them when they're still bursting with exciting fruit but have mellowed into velvety richness. After reaching its zenith, a Zinfandel usually fades away very quickly, loses its distinctive fruit, and can become indistinguishable from any other red wine past its prime.

FOOD AND WINE PAIRINGS

Zinfandel is the best red wine for fried chicken and barbecue. True to its lineage, it is delicious with hangtown fry, an egg-and-oyster dish first whipped up in Placerville, California, for a miner who had struck it rich. It naturally goes with North Beach–style Italian food: pepperoni pizza, linguini with red sauce, cioppino, osso buco. It's a great wine for traditional Caesar salad with anchovies, grilled chops or steak Diane, hearty beef-and-vegetable stews, herb-roasted lamb, and sage and pork. The brambly fruit character of many Zinfandels, particularly Dry Creek bottlings, can counter even fiery chilies in Mexican and Asian dishes and it is very appropriate with Mediterranean cuisine.

It is the sentimental favorite for Thanksgiving for being uniquely American. Despite the traditional mishmash of food flavors on this family occasion, the fruit in the wine will carry the day.

My preferences for cheeses to go with Zinfandel are chèvre with herbs and pepper, dry Monterey Jack, and blues, including Stilton, because Zinfandel can be a Port.

California Syrah

◆◆◆◆◆◆◆

CHARACTER OF THE GRAPE

If any red wine deserves the title of up and coming for the turn of the millennium it should be Syrah. As more and more people turn to red for flavor or health, this variety offers such a range of styles that it is sure to attract many new tasters who look beyond Merlot or Cabernet for wines that tend to be bright in fruit and acid and yet still have bold flavors and textures.

Whether bottled as a 100 percent varietal or blended with Mourvedre, Carignan, or Grenache as is done in the Rhône or with Cabernet Sauvignon as in Australia, Syrah makes an ideal choice for a variety of California *terroirs* because of the state's warm climate.

There are a number of compelling reasons to look to Syrah in 2000. Current winemaking is producing a bright, rich wine that is delicious drunk young, particularly with East-West fusion cuisine. Syrahs are fun to drink on their own, like great Zinfandel—heady and satisfying. They are well priced, certainly compared with Cabernet, and probably the most compelling reason for drinking them is that they are a different flavor.

Syrah originates from the northern Rhône region and was highly prized by the Romans. The steeply terraced, rocky vineyards have hardly changed from what Thomas Jefferson observed from his carriage from Burgundy to Provence. My family drove that same route at the start of every summer in the 1970s. Like Jefferson, I became convinced that wine really had to be a gift because it can prosper in some of the poorest soils in which you can grow hardly anything else. It is a vigorous producer. It does well in relatively cool areas, like the Northern Rhône, as well as warmer zones, more like southern France. The crop size has to be managed to produce wines with intensity. It is considered a late-maturing variety that holds good acidity and is known for its longevity. Most winemakers believe that it is very important to also manage the tannins so that they do not overpower the fruit.

Syrah is not a variety new to California; it was one of the earliest varieties brought to California from France in the 1870s. McDowell Valley in Mendocino County has a beautiful Syrah vineyard from that era. Today there are approximately 1,000 acres of Syrah spread across the face of California from Mendocino south, throughout Napa and Sonoma, into Monterey and the Central Coast, all the way down to San Diego and the Temecula region, and then east and north to the Sierra Nevada foothills. Still, the plantings are dwarfed by the 16,000 acres planted in France and the 30,000 acres in Australia, where the variety, known as Shiraz, is truly the king of Australian red wine. It also shows great promise in South Africa.

There is much confusion about Syrah versus Petite Sirah. Some of the old plantings were Syrah; others were Durif, which is the true grape name of the vines planted as Petite Sirah; and most probably, the old vineyards so highly prized today are really field blends of true Syrah, Carignan, and perhaps some Zinfandel. Unfortunately, most of the historic vineyards are being removed because of old age and are being replaced with "varietally correct" plantings. Call it what you will,

Syrah languished until the early 1980s. The mad rush was to plant Cabernet Sauvignon, Merlot, and Pinot Noir. Joseph Phelps was one of the first to rediscover the potential of Rhône varieties in California, followed by a band of winemakers known as the Rhône Rangers, led by Randall Grahm of Bonny Doon Vineyard.

Randall is a true original. He grew up in Beverly Hills, graduated from University of California Santa Cruz as a philosophy major, then went to work for one of the fancy Beverly Hills wine stores. He is known for being the champion of underrated grapes, making every conceivable wine except Chardonnay and Cabernet and for having a wit like Dorothy Parker's.

For the most part, California wineries have followed a French path stylistically, but recently we are seeing more Syrahs made like Australian Shiraz. The arrival of noted Australian winemakers, such as Daryl Groom of Geyser Peak Winery, who made Penfolds Grange for Penfolds Winery for some years, has brought new ideas and flavors to the variety in California. Their wines tend to be bolder with rich, ripe fruit and lots of extract, though because of technique, the wines are not overly tannic and are therefore delicious when still relatively young.

Another example of the Australian influence is Turley Wine Cellars' Petite Sirah. It is barrel fermented—an Aussie technique for enhancing fruit—and tastes like gently squeezed berries with alcohol. It is the darkest red wine I know, with a wicked, almost macabre black-magenta color around the rim, which makes you think it would be the perfect accompaniment for a Gothic novel or a modern film noir.

There is no one style or flavor of California Syrah. As with all grapes, a template slowly emerges in each climate. In warmer areas—Dry Creek, Alexander Valley, the Sierra Nevada foothills, and the hill regions of Napa and Mendocino—the variety shows a lot of blackberry fruit that is often jammy with licorice and cassis. Cooler regions like the Central Coast and parts of Monterey often exhibit more peppercorn in their fruit. The oft-mentioned barnyard or gamy flavors of Syrah can be found in wines from all climates and is probably a slightly reduced character, which comes from the winemaking.

If we start in the north, my first choice is McDowell Valley Vineyards east of Hopland in Mendocino County. With its own unique appellation and one of the oldest and largest Syrah plantings in the state, this family has made a true commitment not only to 100 percent Syrah wines but also to a blend with other Rhône grapes called Le Tresor. Their 1995 Estate Bottled Syrah (Old Vine) is full of blackberry, pepper, and allspice concentrated in a deep, rich body. Le Tresor has the same intense fruit blended with earthy tones and a broader palate. Also from Mendocino is Fetzer Vineyards' Bonterra Syrah.

Sonoma County has a number of fine producers and some great old vineyards particularly in Dry Creek, the Russian River Valley, and the Sonoma Valley. I have already mentioned Geyser Peak's Shiraz. The '94 Reserve is a stunning example of great fruit with supple texture. The '95 Sonoma has more earthy character blended with great fruit and a powerful structure.

Lou Preston of Preston Vineyards has a lovely Estate Syrah from Dry Creek, which is fragrant and very elegant. Tom Dehlinger makes a gutsy old-vine Syrah that begs for aging. Philip Staley and Toad Hollow both make delicious blends that are wonderful for early drinking.

Old-fashioned Petite Sirah is an endangered species in Sonoma. Only 300 acres remain from what formerly

Personal Recommendations

EXPENSIVE

Bonny Doon Vineyard (Santa Cruz)
Turley Wine Cellars (Napa Valley)

MODERATE

Eberle (Paso Robles)
Fife Petite Sirah (Mendocino)
Foxen (Santa Ynez Valley)
Geyser Peak Winery Shiraz (Alexander Valley)
McDowell Valley Vineyards Syrah (Mendocino)
Joseph Phelps Vineyards (Napa Valley)
Qupé (Santa Barbara)
Zaca Mesa Winery "Z" Cuvée (Santa Barbara)

INEXPENSIVE

Foppiano Wine Co. Petite Sirah (Sonoma County)
Forest Glen Shiraz (California)
R. H. Phillips "EXP" (Yolo County)

must have been thousands. It grows best in the eastern reaches of the Russian River Valley, a comparatively warm basin, close to the western boundary of the Alexander Valley. The old-style wines can be tough when young (though that's also changing with fashion and technology), but a mature wine from Foppiano Wine Co., Christopher Creek Winery, or Hop Kiln Winery has a scent of fine leather and crushed rose petals.

In Napa, Joseph Phelps's Vin du Mistral is a particular favorite. Winemaker Craig Williams has a way with the variety and he attains great depth of fruit while still keeping it elegant. The '94 Swanson is exceptional and

Sean Thackery's Orion has a stellar concentration that is worth the very difficult search to find a bottle. All of Thackery's wines are named after constellations, though his winery is little more than a rough-hewn backyard barn.

Santa Cruz has a number of fine, small wineries making Syrah, sourcing fruit from around the state, but none with such a touch as that of Bonny Doon Vineyard. The Central Coast also deserves attention. The variety is grown from King City to Santa Barbara in a variety of different microclimates, from very warm Paso Robles to cool Tepusquet Vineyard in Cambria. My particular favorites are Eberle, Qupé, and Zaca Mesa Winery, which have served as a training ground for many of Santa Barbara's best winemakers.

After many years of prospecting with a number of varieties, it now appears that Syrah works well in a developing grape-growing region east of San Diego. And the Sierra Nevada foothills are just beginning to show how they are capable of making big Syrah wines that are often jammy and full of extract and body. The wines of Edmunds St. John and Sierra Vista Winery are outstanding examples.

WHEN TO DRINK

The Syrah variety is noted for its longevity. You can find 1984 McDowell Valley Vineyards and Qupé on some California wine lists, but they can be delicious when young, because of modern winemaking techniques, in a heady, gutsy, intensely fruity Zinfandel kind of way.

COMPARISONS WITH FRANCE AND AUSTRALIA

For some reason, the world long ignored the wines of the Rhône Valley. They weren't fashionable and

Vintage Chart

1990 A steady, hot vintage. The Syrahs are deeply flavored and ready to drink.

1992 Another consistently warm year with a generally big crop and soft wines that are ready to drink.

1994 Generally regarded by all producers as great—the best of the decade—because it was a long, warm season with fairly low yields. The Syrahs have intense fruit and body and will be long lived. McDowell Valley Vineyards made its first Port with Syrah in '94.

1995 This was a warm vintage, again with low yields, which always benefit intensity.

tended to be massive and tannic. You wouldn't serve Hermitage at a Paris dinner party unless the wine was at least 30 years old. Bordeaux and Burgundy were *it*, until their prices reached such heights that most wine buyers became more flexible and venturesome. Likewise, California winemakers were stuck on producing Cabernet and Chardonnay.

Times change. Tastes change. A greater awareness of the Rhône's fine wines, coupled with more sophisticated winemaking and a dramatic change in taste toward richer, fruitier wines, has brought Syrah to the forefront. Fabulous wines from the northern Rhône, especially those of Marcel Guigal and his single-vineyard Côte Rôtie, have inspired a more elegant style, with more intrinsic fruit. Then there are the Rhône-style Syrahs with leather and barnyard on the nose and spicy pepper on the palate.

A highly regarded family operation, E. Guigal has always made good wines, but they seem now to get better and better. Perhaps this is the result of success, often the case in winemaking, a kind of self-fulfilling prophecy driven by wine writers and consumer demand, leading to more recognition and higher prices, which pay for more new barrels and other costly improvements.

Australian Shiraz is unbridled, intense, dark berry fruit with a lush, supple mouth feel and a long, clean, racy finish. Those from Penfolds, Henschke & Co., and Clarendon Hill Winery are amazing examples of their style, and you want to drink them as soon as you can get your hands on them. They are typically blended with 10 to 20 percent Cabernet Sauvignon. Part of their appeal is that they are very richly oaked.

California Syrahs seem to fall in the middle. Ours have a heightened sense of fruit like Australia's, but with less oak and some restraint, which is more akin to France's. And our blends range from having a small amount of Viognier like a Côte Rôti or a dollop of Cabernet like the Australians' Syrahs.

FOOD AND WINE PAIRINGS

I recommend Syrah with robust dishes like stews, cassoulets, ragouts, pastas, couscous, pizzas, hearty soups, and barbecued steaks and chops. In Australia and the Rhône, people love Syrah with leg of lamb. It goes beautifully with grilled summer vegetables and fresh, oven-roasted, or sun-dried tomatoes, and it has an affinity for nutty flavors, such as wild and brown rices.

It is delicious with peppery and garlicky Szechuan spices. It does not do well with salty food.

Cheese suggestions include fresh chèvre, dry Sonoma Jack, Port Salut, Coulommiers, Brie, double and triple creams such as Muenster, Havarti, or mild and nutty cheeses such as Emmenthal.

A favorite winter combination of mine is Syrah with roasted chestnuts.

California Italian

HISTORY: SANGIOVESE, NEBBIOLO, BARBERA, AND DOLCETTO

There is a long history of growing Italian grapes in America, beginning with Thomas Jefferson's experiments in Virginia. Jefferson's first personal investment in a vineyard was called La Colle—on a hill adjacent to Monticello—planted by an Italian, Fillipo Mazzei. Mazzei came from an established Tuscan wine family, nobles since the fourteenth century, who continue to produce superb Chianti Classico at Castello di Fonterutoli near Siena. Their early American venture failed: Cavalry horses trampled the vineyards. Mazzei went on to become a statesman and diplomat, and Virginia's best results so far have been with white wine.

A later wave of Italian immigrants brought to California a natural love of wine and a basic, practically inborn knowledge of how to grow and produce it. Many of Sonoma's leading wine families got their start when their great-grandfathers gave up digging for gold. The story goes that Samuele Sebastiani, rather than work in a rock quarry, sold homemade wine by the tin cup from a horse-drawn wagon to the other thirsty, predominantly Italian workers. Of course today, Sebastiani Vineyards is California's sixth largest winery, producing over 7 million cases a year. Most of these families long ago switched to producing Chardonnay and Cabernet Sauvignon—just like everyone else—though some, like the Seghesios, have gone back to focusing on Italian varietals.

Robert Pepi deserves special recognition because just about everybody growing Sangiovese today got some of their original vine cuttings from him. Well into his eighties now, he gave bud wood (the grafting material) to "anybody who asked," he says. "Sangiovese is so wonderful, I just wanted to see it propagated."

SANGIOVESE HISTORY

Sangiovese is the principal grape in Tuscany. Its history reaches back to the Etruscans. It has a sweet-tart flavor like cherries and is more delicate than Cabernet Sauvignon. I often perceive a kind of sweetness—almost like a drop of fine, aged Balsamic—that for me distinguishes rich Italian reds from Cabernet. I've also heard this taste described as the smell of lilies. The lily happens to be the symbol of Florence. As a category, I put Sangiovese somewhere between Pinot Noir and Zinfandel. It has a brightness and acidity that reminds me of Pinot Noir, but a fullness and spiciness that is more akin to Zinfandel.

Interest in Sangiovese is growing in California. One reason is probably our food. So much of California's orientation is toward the direct, bright flavors of Italian cooking, which naturally invites Sangiovese. It has become a very hot item on restaurant wine lists—suddenly it seems that everyone has jumped on the bandwagon. There was only a handful of producers in 1990, but today there are almost 100. Still, there are fewer than 1,000 acres of the grape in California, compared with 80,000 acres of Cabernet Sauvignon. Little of it leaves the state. It is an expressive grape in the sense that it can truly embody the personality of the place where it is grown, whereas a grape like Cabernet tends to dominate. Cabernet has such a strong stamp it can sometimes overwhelm the taste of the land. The challenge is making a Sangiovese all our own and not just imitation Italian, or worse, some kind of homogeneous international style that could come from anywhere. As with all wines, the finest Sangiovese wines reflect not only good grapes but also the hillside on which they are grown and the personalities of the people behind them.

Planting Sangiovese in California was considered very pioneering in the late 1980s. Bud wood was very hard to come by. Some vintners resorted to "suitcase selections" smuggled past customs after a trip to Italy, which had its risks not only legally but because they could have brought in unwanted pests or disease. Forrest, my husband, once tried to import a few cuttings from Tuscany, but not one survived. The result is that most of us in California are working with one predominant clone of Sangiovese, whereas most of the Italian vineyards are a mix of many different clones. Even the Italians disagree on whether that matters. At a recent conference, a top Tuscany enologist (expert in the science of wines and winemaking) begged the question "What is a clone?" We have no way of measuring whether a certain taste or characteristic is genetically inscribed or if it is merely one of nature's lovely quirks in the vineyard that makes it distinctive. At the same symposium, I heard Marchese Piero Antinori, whose family has been making wine for 26 generations, and young Vittorio Frescobaldi, whose family has been involved with winemaking for 650 years, give two diametrically opposed views on whether density planting (closer spacing) makes the vines more or less vigorous with more or less intense fruit, which simply tells me that despite their families' long history, we are all, as winemakers, on the same page.

Current wisdom is that all wines started getting better in the 1960s, simultaneous with a wine revolution in Bordeaux led by Emil Peynaud and in California with Robert Mondavi. It started in Tuscany with the release of Sassicaia, made by Marchesi Mario Incisa della Rocchetta, and Piero Antinori's Tignanello, in the mid-1970s. Both were revivals of a nineteenth-century practice of blending a small amount of Cabernet Sauvignon with Sangiovese. Both were also part of a desire to experiment and compete in the international wine market, creating a separate category from old-style Chianti.

Traditional Chianti producers made their break in 1982, restructuring the *Denominazione di Origine Controllata* (DOC) laws to give themselves more freedom in the composition and style of their wines. They increased the amount of Sangiovese and lowered the amount of white wine grapes in the blend, making Chianti more of a red wine, darker in color and more full bodied.

Now there is Chianti 2000, a project initiated by Chianti Classico Consorzio to upgrade the vineyards, focusing more on *terroir* and cultivation than winemaking. Even the Italians use the French term *terroir* to express all the various elements, such as soil and climate, that add up to the taste of the land.

The prevalent opinion of California Sangiovese is that we have a long way to go. At one point, in the early 1990s, it was considered a new, hot prospect, judging by the dramatic increase in bud wood being sold by the nurseries. Using the same yardstick, a sharp decrease in demand for Sangiovese bud wood five years later attests to difficulties with the grape.

Piero Antinori has a massive investment in 110 acres devoted to Sangiovese on Atlas Peak, the highest, steepest, rockiest, most easterly vineyard of Napa. Though too suave to express it openly, Antinori has to have been disappointed by the early vintages. One reason may be that Sangiovese comes into its own only when the vines are mature. All young vines have a tendency to want to produce more fruit than they should when they are between five and 10 years old. With our lack of real experience with Sangiovese, it's not surprising that we Californians ended up with many wines' having an overcropped character—lean, tomato-like, and rather weak in color. That is rapidly changing not only with the further age of the vines but also with much more rigorous thinning and superior winemaking techniques that concentrate more on color and fruit.

Another fact we've learned is that Sangiovese is as difficult to cultivate as Pinot Noir and just as site specific. It appears that certain locations with poorer, well-drained soils are the best sites for this variety. The west-facing slopes of the Alexander Valley, the east side of Napa, northern Mendocino, and of course the Sierra Nevada foothills seem to be the locations where this variety will really prosper. It is also a variety very subject to sunburn on the young fruit, so trellising is an essential ingredient to good grape growing.

The other issue with Sangiovese is blending. At Iron Horse Vineyards, Forrest initially blended with Cabernet and Swanson is blending with a small amount of Syrah. Much of this type of experimenting will continue to go on for some time, though Forrest feels that when the good vineyards have matured, we will see more 100 percent Sangiovese that is dark in color, is brimming with dark bing cherry fruit, is supple on the palate, and has the variety's characteristic crisp finish.

My favorites to try are those from Chappellet and Ferrari-Carrano Vineyards & Winery and Shafer Vineyards' blend of Sangiovese and Cabernet, which they call Firebreak, because the vineyard was actually first planted to be a firebreak for the main house.

Staglin Family Vineyard makes a delicious wine called Stagliano, recalling the family heritage. Atlas Peak's best release so far is its '95 Reserve. Robert Mondavi Winery has a separate line of "Cal-Ital" wines, La Famiglia di Robert Mondavi, as well as a joint venture in Montalcino with Marchesi de' Frescobaldi called Luce. Even Gallo has started importing wines from Italy.

The thirst for all things Italian is not limited to California. Gary Figgins in Walla Walla, Washington, famous for Cabernet and Merlot, named his winery Leonetti Cellars after his grandparents and made his first Sangiovese in 1995 as a tribute to them. But I think the success and acclaim of the super-Tuscans and

Personal Recommendations for Sangiovese

EXPENSIVE

Ferrari-Carano Vineyards & Winery Siena (Sonoma County)

Flora Springs Wine Co. (Napa Valley)

Shafer Vineyards Firebreak (Napa)

Staglin Family Vineyard Stagliano (Napa Valley)

Swanson (Napa Valley)

MODERATE

Acorn (Russian River Valley)

Chappellet (Napa Valley)

Clos du Val Wine Co. (Napa Valley)

Dalla Valle Vineyard Pietra Santa (Napa Valley)

INEXPENSIVE

Bonny Doon Vineyard (Monterey County)

the wines of Angelo Gaja of Italy's Piedmont region may have been as inspiring to American winemakers as the search for immigrant roots.

WHEN TO DRINK SANGIOVESE

Most Sangiovese are meant to be drunk after three or four years. They are fruity, almost citrusy when young. More spiciness comes out with age. After seven or eight years, some will last and some will fade. Even such expensive super-Tuscans as Sassicaia, Solaia, and Ornellaia in a superlative vintage like '90 are ready to drink now.

California has been making too little Sangiovese for too short a time to develop much of a track record, obviating any kind of vintage chart. Like so many other red wines in California, it seems that each new vintage brings greater and greater results. The learning curve is still so steep that it exceeds the impact of vintage variation. Certainly, '94 was excellent for the variety, but having tasted a fair number of '95s and some '96s, I would say the best is yet to come.

COMPARISONS OF CALIFORNIA SANGIOVESE WITH TUSCAN WINES

California Sangiovese tends to be more opulent, fleshy, supple, and approachable and to have more fruit intensity and softer tannins. Tuscan wines are less fruity, firmer, much leaner, and more defined by brightness and nerve. The acidity tends to be higher and more volatile in Italian wines, which goes back to the grapes as well as to a long tradition of making wine a certain way. Italian wines are made for food; more so than any other wines, they need to be tasted with food to be fully appreciated.

FOOD AND SANGIOVESE WINE PAIRINGS

Sangiovese is made for uncomplicated, uncontrived, simply delicious country food—Mama's cooking—such as handmade pastas, lamb and white beans, a juicy Florentine steak with braised fennel, and spinach and cannellini beans. Ironically, a big oaky Sangiovese doesn't go very well with pizza, which needs a higher-acid wine like traditional Chiantis, which are blended with white wines for freshness and acidity.

Italians still seem to prefer wines of a region with the food of that region, perhaps out of pride or a wish to preserve tradition. Highly regarded American writer Waverly Root expressed a similar bias, asking, "Who would think of drinking a fine Médoc with a dish of spaghetti?" This comment has to be taken in the context of when it was written. His book, *The Food of Italy,* considered a classic, was published in 1971. But still, the tremendous cross-cultural experimentation with food that we see in America doesn't happen much in Italy, and although I agree that the traditional food and wine combinations have the special savor of history and culture, I also feel that they are not the only possibilities.

For once, here is something that shows the French to be more open-minded: The Bordeaux Council advertises its wines as appropriate with pizza (perhaps because the food of Bordeaux is so uninspiring). I love Pinot Noir with carpaccio of Portobello mushrooms with a little olive oil and pepper on lavosh bread.

I find Sangiovese as food-versatile as Pinot Noir, combining bright fruit, zesty acidity, soft and finely textured tannin, and earthy undertones that work wonderfully with rich, wood-grilled salmon, boneless rack of lamb and roasted elephant garlic, and tournedos of beef capped with béarnaise sauce. Cookbook writer Eileen Yin-Fei Lo recommends Sangiovese with Asian-style steamed orange beef.

Sangiovese is naturally at home with Tuscan Pecorino and cacciotta and it's usually first choice with true Parmesan (parmigiano reggiano), produced in the region of Emilia-Romagna but deemed best with great Sangiovese.

NEBBIOLO HISTORY

Nebbiolo, the grape in Barolo and Barbaresco, has yet to successfully take root outside Piedmont. The few I would recommend from California are the Nebbiolo from Sanford and Jim Clendenen's Il Podere dell'Olivos, both from the Central Coast, and Seghesio from Sonoma. Some of these are direct sale only.

Nebbiolo is very difficult to grow. The vineyards around Alba are small, planted like patchwork, and even steeper than Burgundy. There, the width of a ditch can make a vast difference in quality. It's a slow-ripening grape, which is why Piedmont growers say south-facing slopes, catching the most sun and where the snow melts first, historically provide the best fruit. A good piece of consumer advice is to look for the words *sori* and *bricco* on the Italian label, which mean "south-facing" and "hilltop," respectively, in the local dialect.

Nebbiolo wines are dark, rich, complex, elegant mouthfuls of tannin with ripe, spicy black fruit, a smoky nose, and the scent of rose petals. They become slightly amber in color with age, developing more power and such scents like truffles, chocolate, and pine tar and sometimes retaining a faintly bitter zest even at their peak. Piedmont is near the Alps, so traditionally the wines tend to be robust and warming.

WHEN TO DRINK NEBBIOLO

The old argument with Nebbiolo wines, i.e., Barolos, was to let them age for 20 years because they were so tannic, but now the wines are made so you can drink them younger, just as we do Bordeaux or Cabernet Sauvignon. The producers say nine to ten years is optimum aging in a good vintage. Lighter vintages can be enjoyed within two or three years. They are not for the faint of heart but are still more gentle than Randy Dunn's current vintage of Cabernet.

FOOD AND NEBBIOLO WINE PAIRINGS

Nebbiolo naturally goes with the comfort food of Piedmont: veal carpaccio with slivers of white truffles, homemade sausages, lentil soup, ravioli stuffed with ricotta and sage, bolito misto, roasts and braised meats with creamy mashed potatoes, Fontina fondue, and a flaky, aged toma.

I have been warned against spicy food with Nebbiolo because it makes the wine taste thin and bitter.

BARBERA HISTORY

A handful of Californians are growing Barbera, which used to produce a rather rough, ordinary wine, but it is becoming more refined and successful in Italy with new winemaking techniques. Often, a top-quality effort with a second-tier grape will be the better buy, just as rising star wines are more affordable before they become famous. California Barberas include Mondavi, Il Podere dell'Olivos, and Seghesio. Sebastiani Vineyards has been making a Barbera since its inception in 1904.

DOLCETTO HISTORY

Dolcetto, also a grape from Piedmont, makes light, fruity, pleasing, everyday, and theoretically inexpensive wine. Kent Rasmussen makes a gorgeously rich, fragrant Dolcetto that he bottles in blue glass, and Acorn, based in Healdsburg, produces a late-harvest version.

My favorite Italian wine to drink with a bowl of simple spaghetti or pizza is Dolcetto, often compared to Beaujolais because it's a fruity young everyday wine, though Dolcettos tend to have more structure and depth.

A purist combines young cherrylike Dolcetto with a sweet, blue-veined Gorgonzola, as both the wine and the cheese come from Piedmont. This is the same logic as matching sweet Sauternes with Roquefort.

Rosés

◆◆◆◆◆◆◆

THE HEIGHT OF SOPHISTICATION

It is now considered the height of sophistication to recognize the difference between Rosés and blush wines and to take the position that residual sugar in wine, though not to my taste, is far from the end of the world.

Crisp, dry, easy-drinking, uncomplicated, happy Rosés come from all over the world. (My husband Forrest and I had a delicious Moroccan Rosé—unexpected from a Muslim country—with hot and spicy fish tagine and couscous at a trendy restaurant called Momo's in London.) They come in an array of colors, from slightly tinged, pale, peony pink to coppery orange to watermelon red. And they're made from all kinds of red-wine grapes—Cabernet, Pinot Noir, Zinfandel, of course, Sangiovese and, most traditionally, from Grenache, Mourvedre, Cinsault, and the other varietals of southern France.

The universal factor is that they're light, lower in alcohol than other wines, and thirst quenching. You drink them like water. They make you dream of sun-drenched places where the sky is enormously blue and your glass is never empty. Rosés are good for the psyche.

Simi Winery makes a Rosé of Cabernet that is always fresh, fruity, and faultless.

Saintsbury's Vincent Vin Gris, Etude's Rosé, and Sanford Rosé are all Blanc de Pinot Noirs, which tend to be more elegant, crisp, and delicate.

What can be said about white Zinfandel? Its history could be a Harvard MBA case study in marketing. It was essentially an invention born of necessity when vintners found themselves with an excess of Zinfandel grapes and no buyers. Sutter Home Winery is generally credited with creating white Zinfandel; it is still a thriving business. The trend now is to make white Zinfandels a little less sweet. Beringer Vineyards is doing a very good job of this, and I have seen Mondavi Woodbridge white Zinfandel offered by the glass at some very fine restaurants. Why? Because even though it may not be ubiquitous as it was in the 1980s, it still is being sucked down by more wine drinkers than Cabernet Sauvignon is.

Pedroncelli Winery's Zinfandel Rosé, though off dry, stands apart for having more character than typical blush wine does.

Lately, I have become infatuated with Rosato di Sangiovese. We at Iron Horse have one, as does Swanson, made by bleeding about 20 percent of the newly fermented wine from the barrel to make the remaining red more intense and bottling what has been drawn off as an intensely fruity, early drinking rosé.

Joseph Phelps Vineyards' Vin du Mistral is inspired by Provence and Bonny Doon Vineyard's Vin Gris de Cigar is Randall Grahm's take on the Rhône.

For me, the best Rosés have bubbles in them, as in Sparkling Wine or Champagne. Most people look at pink bubbly and assume it's going to be sweet, but Rosé Champagnes, like Dom Pérignon Rosé, can be the driest, most expensive, most exclusive of all bubblies. The color is achieved two ways—either by adding Pinot Noir still wine to the blend or by letting the Pinot Noir juice sit on the skins. French Rosé Champagnes tend to be pale salmon or onion-skin color, but in California, we make ours to be much more intense and vibrant, probably because we also produce Blanc de Noirs, which hardly exist in France. A Blanc de Noir is typically made from 100 percent Pinot Noir grapes and comes out a pink-gold color.

Personal Recommendations

MODERATE

Gloria Ferrer Blanc de Noirs NV (Carneros)

INEXPENSIVE

Bonny Doon Vineyard Vin Gris de Cigar (Central Coast)
Domaine Chandon Blanc de Noirs NV (Napa Valley)
Etude Pinot Noir Rosé (Napa Valley)
McDowell Valley Vineyards Grenache Rosé (Mendocino)
Joseph Phelps Vineyards Vin du Mistral (Napa Valley)
Saintsbury Vincent Vin Gris (Napa Valley)
Swanson Rosato (Napa Valley)

WHEN TO DRINK

There's no such thing as a vintage chart for Rosés. Usually they're meant to be drunk within a year. Again, Sparkling Wines, or Champagnes, are the exception because the very best are vintage, which means not only that the grapes come from one year, but that by law in France, the wine has been aged for at least three years with the yeast in the bottle. This caliber of Rosé can easily last another three years on the cork.

One of the main attributes of Rosés is their freshness. How California Rosés compare with world-renowned Tavel, Domaine Tempier's Bandol Rosé, or Domaines Ott from Provence seems like a moot point, as even the most expensive French Rosés taste best in their place of origin.

FOOD AND WINE PAIRINGS

All Rosés should be chilled. On a hot day, nothing is more refreshing with grilled chicken, grilled sausages, pasta salads, and fresh tomato salsas. I would pick a Rosé to go with a roast beef sandwich, chicken fajitas, or a tuna burger.

The dry ones are delicious with every type of Mediterranean food from the south of France, Italy, Spain, Morocco, and Turkey: crudités, bouillabaisse, grilled fresh sardines, tomato, onion and olive foccacias, paella, tabbouleh salad, stuffed grape leaves, and swordfish kebabs.

Off-dry styles go beautifully with Chinese food, especially sweet-and-sour dishes such as moo shu pork because of the hoisin sauce, which gives sweetness to an otherwise uncomplicated match.

White Zinfandel may be one of the few wines I would recommend with a Big Mac (because of the special sauce), a hot dog with catsup, or turkey on rye with Russian dressing.

I recommend Blanc de Noirs Sparkling with smoked salmon, popcorn shrimp, thinly sliced proscuitto, frittata, and anything to do with mushrooms, such as grilled Portobello mushrooms or wild mushroom risotto. This wine would be one of my choices for sushi. I would serve Blanc de Noir with asparagus and cold poached salmon for a pretty, light luncheon; a New Orleans gumbo dinner with rice and potato salad; and—any time of day or night—with chocolate-dipped strawberries.

I love Brut Rosé with fried oysters, spinach salad, or spinach soufflé; with a beautiful piece of grilled tuna or sushi-quality tuna tartar; with duck or a veal chop. One of my favorite food-and-wine combinations is Brut Rosé and steak. I even serve it in a big Burgundy glass, so you get this bath of bubbles down your throat. It makes me feel like I'm Diamond Jim Brady.

I know one wine expert who believes you should always drink Rosé Sparkling or Champagne with fried chicken and many who think it's the best match with barbecue.

Epilogue: Looking Forward

I see many happy vintages ahead. Granted, I'm an optimist, but wine is realistically one of the few things in life that I can promise will continue to improve. Nineteen ninety-nine was my husband's twenty-ninth vintage, and he's the first to say he's just getting the hang of it. He promises me he hasn't peaked yet. If nothing else, I can assure you that what we have in the cellar will send us into the next millennium with a bang.

Wines will continue to improve because winemaking techniques will continue to evolve as we learn more about the vineyards. California will never have disasters like 1983 or even as bad as 1989 again. Even Europe won't have the washouts they used to.

We'll have phylloxera behind us—at least this particular biotype. It's been an incredibly long haul since damage was first detected in 1980. The silver lining to phylloxera is that so much vineyard land has been upgraded. We know so much more about where to plant, what to plant, different trellising systems, and the spacing of the vines than we did in the '70s when most of the vineyards were originally planted. Those who bit the bullet and replanted early now have new vineyards finally coming into their own.

Generally, everyone feels that the wines from these new plantings are superior. Wineries like Iron Horse Vineyards and Acacia are replanting even without the impetus of phylloxera—for fear of being at a competitive disadvantage if we don't. And not every inch has been replanted to Merlot. Henry Wendt of Quivia actually pulled out Merlot in favor of Sauvignon Blanc, being one of those rare birds not to follow fashion.

Paul Draper of Ridge Vineyards has started regenerating his favorite old Zinfandel vineyards, using cuttings from the old vines to repropagate specific clones and particular field blends. There are fewer than 1,000 acres of century-old vines to work with, but the early results show they can be "brought back" through a new generation.

Meanwhile, more and more Americans are becoming interested in wine. What else are you going to drink with a nice dinner? France, Italy, and Spain each import about 5 percent of their wines, compared with the 18 percent brought into the United States, but I think the U.S. percentage will level out to be the same as that of other wine-producing countries.

On the other side of the coin, I feel very comfortable in predicting that competition will grow every year—from everywhere—which always leads to higher quality. And I can further assure you that winemakers have a good sense of history and will pour everything they've got into making 2000 special.

With that said, here is one last piece of consumer advice: If you are looking for an everyday drinking wine—something to go with salads, hamburgers, or various pastas—I recommend a good, clean, medium-bodied, dry, smooth American Zinfandel.

Index

*An * denotes a Personal Recommendation wine*

Acacia, 27, 101–02
  Pinot Noir*, 40, 43, 49
Acorn
  Dolcetto, 94
  Sangiovese*, 89
Adelsheim, David, 48
Adelsheim Pinot Noir, 48
Aging of wines, 7, 10, 18, 23, 31, 36, 39, 42, 50, 52, 55, 59
Alexander Valley, 18–19, 77, 88
  Vineyards Cabernet, 19
Andrew Will Merlot*, 61, 62
Antinori, Piero, 86, 87
Apex Merlot, 62
A. Rafanelli Zinfandel*, 71
Araujo, Bart and Daphne, 24
Araujo Estate Wines, 13
  Cabernet, 24
Archery Summit Pinot Noir, 47, 48
Arrowood, Dick, 12–13
Arrowood, 20
  Cabernet and Merlot, 3
Atlas Peak, 25
  Sangiovese, 87–88, 89
Au Bon Climat Pinot Noir, 42, 43
Australia, 19, 31, 58, 77
  Shiraz, 76, 77, 82
Bancroft Ranch, 12
Bannister Zinfandel*, 71
Barbera, 93
  Il Podere dell'Olivos, 93
  Mondavi, 93
  Sebastiani, 93
  Seghesio, 93
Barrett, Bo, 25
Barrett, Heidi Peterson, 13, 25
Beaulieu, 22
  Georges de Latour Cabernet, 23
  Tapestry* Cabernet, 28
Beaux Frères Pinot Noir, 45, 47, 48
Beckstoffer, Andy, 23
Benz, Christina, 19
Benziger Merlot*, 61
Beringer, 12
  Cabernet, 30
  Merlot*, 59, 61
  Napa Ridge Cabernet*, 12, 28
  Napa Ridge Pinot Noir*, 49
  Private Reserve, 12
  white Zinfandel, 96
Bernardus, Marinus* Cabernet, 28
Bettane, Michel, 30

Biale Zinfandel, 69
Bien Nacido Pinot Noir, 41
Blackstone Merlot*, 61
Bonny Doon, 13
Sangiovese*, 89
Syrah*, 77, 79, 80
Vin Gris de Cigar Rosé*, 96, 97
Bordeaux, 3, 5, 6, 9, 11, 15–16, 31, 58
classification 1855, 30
comparison, California Cabernet, 29–31
comparison, American Merlot, 62–63
cost, 29, 30, 31
wine revolution, 86–87
Brick House Pinot Noir, 47
Brounstein, Al, 18
Bulgarian Merlot, 58
Burgundy, 9, 11–12, 30, 38, 42, 50, 51
best shippers, 50
comparison, Pinot Noir, 49–55
price, 51, 55
Byron Pinot Noir*, 49

Cabernet Sauvignon, 6, 16
acres of, 85
aging of, 31, 36, 39
Araujo Estate, 24
Arrowood, 3
Beaulieu Tapestry*, 22, 23, 28
Bernardus, Marinus*, 28
Carmenet, 20, 27
Caymus, 17
Château St. Jean "Cinq Cepages"*, 28
Château Souverain*, 19, 28
changes in, 32
Cinnabar*, 26, 28
comparison, Bordeaux, 29–31
Corison*, 28
Cornerstone*, 28
cost, 15, 17
Counterpoint, 20
Diamond Creek, 17–18
Dominus Estate, 25
Dunn, 36
"dust," 22, 23
food and, 36–37
Freemark Abbey, 22
Georges de Latour, 23
Geyser Peak*, 28
grape, 15
Groth, 17, 23
Heitz Martha's Vineyard, 17
Hess Select*, 28
Jordan, 17
Kathryn Kennedy, 26
Kenwood, 20
Louis Martini Monte Rosso*, 21, 28
Mondavi, 17, 23
Murphy-Goode*, 28
Napa Ridge*, 28
Opus One, 17, 25
personal recommendations, 28
Pride Mountain*, 28
Randy Dunn, 22, 93
Rodney Strong*, 28

Screaming Eagle, 13, 24
Shafer, 22
Silver Oak, 17, 18
Simi Reserve*, 28
Spottswoode*, 28
Stag's Leap, 17, 22
"ten year magic," 3
Terra Rosa*, 20, 28
vintage chart, 33
when to drink, 36
Whitehall Lane*, 28
young, gentle, 31–32
Calera Pinot Noir, 43, 48, 55
California wine, 1, 3, 9, 101–02. *See also specific regions; wines; wineries*
blends, 13, 58
Merlot in, 58–60, 102
phylloxera in, 9, 21, 24, 32, 101–02
varietals, 13
vineyards and vintners, 12–14
Camp Meeting Ridge Pinot Noir, 41
Campbell, Patrick, 20
Canoe Ridge
Cabernet, 27
Merlot*, 61
Pinot Noir, 43
Cappelli, Marco, 24
Carmel Valley, 27
Carmenet Cabernet, 20, 27, 43
Carneros, 39, 40, 51, 52, 54, 60
Carneros Creek Winery Pinot Noir, 40
Caymus Cabernet, 17, 22, 23, 30
Central Coast, 41, 52, 54, 78, 80, 92. *See also* Santa Barbara
Chabot, 12
Chalk Hill Estate Cabernet, 25
Chalone Pinot Noir, 42–43
Group, 43
Vineyard, 27, 42
Chappellet Sangiovese*, 88, 89
Chardonnay, 42
Château Haut-Brion, 4
Château Lafite, 16, 31
-Rothschild, 43
Château Lafleur de Gay, 62
Château Les Pins, 30, 62
Chateau Montelena Cabernet, 25, 30
Château Mouton-Rothschild Cabernet, 16, 25
Château Pétrus, 25, 59, 62, 63
Chateau Potelle* Zinfandel, 71
Château St. Jean, 13
"Cinq Cepages" Cabernet, 28
Chateau Ste. Michelle
Cabernet, 27
Merlot, 62
Château Souverain Cabernet*, 28
Chianti, 87
Cinnabar Cabernet*, 26, 28
Clarendon Hill Shiraz, 82
Clendenen, Jim, 42, 92

Cline Zinfandel*, 71
Clos du Bois
Cabernet, 19
Merlot, 60
Clos du Val
Cabernet, 22
Sangiovese*, 89
Zinfandel, 71
Colgin, Ann, 13
Colgin Cellars, 13
Columbia Crest
Cabernet, 27
Merlot*, 57, 61
Columbia Milestone Merlot, 62
Columbia Winery Merlot*, 61
Corison, Cathy, 13
Corison Wines Cabernet*, 28
Cornerstone Cabernet*, 26, 28
Cristom's Marjorie and Mount Jefferson Pinot Noir, 48

Dalla Valle, 13
Pietra Santa Sangiovese*, 89
Daniel, John, 25
Davenport, Margaret, 19
Dehlinger, Tom, 78
Dehlinger
Pinot Noir*, 40, 49
Syrah, 78
Delille Cabernet, 29
DeLoach
Pinot Noir, 40
Zinfandel*, 71
Diamond Creek Cabernet, 17–18
Disney, Lillian, 22
Doerner, Steve, 48
Dolcetto, 93–94
Domaine Carneros Pinot Noir, 44
Domaine Chandon Blanc de Noirs Rosé*, 97
Domaine de la Romanée Conti, 30, 43
Domaine Drouhin Pinot Noir, 48
La Forêt, 55
Laurene, 47
Domaine Dujac, 43
Dominus Estate Cabernet, 25–26
Draper, Paul, 102
Drouhin, Joseph, 46–47, 55
Drouhin, Veronique, 47
Duckhorn Merlot*, 59, 60, 61, 64
Dunn, Randy, 22
Dunn Vineyards
Cabernet, 22, 93
Pinot Noir, 36
Dutton, Warren, 44

Eberle Syrah*, 79, 80
Ecole 41 Cabernet, 29
Edmunds St. John Syrah, 80
Edna Valley
Cabernet, 27
Pinot Noir, 43
Eisele Cabernet, 24
Eisele, Milton, 24
El Molino Pinot Noir, 44

Estancia Merlot*, 61
Etude (Tony Soter's), 13
  Pinot Noir, 43
  Rosé*, 95, 97

Far Niente Cabernet, 23
Ferrari-Carano
  Cabernet, 19
  Merlot*, 61
  Sangiovese*, 88, 89
Fetzer's Bonterra Syrah, 78
Fife
  Petite Sirah*, 79
  Redhead Zin*, 71
Figgins, Gary, 89
Flora Springs Sangiovese*, 89
Flowers Pinot Noir, 41
Foppiano Petite Sirah*, 79
Forest Glen Shiraz*, 79
Foxen Syrah*, 79
Franciscan Oakville Estate Cabernet, 23
Freemark Abbey Cabernet Bosche, 22
Frescobaldi, Vittorio, 86

Gaja, Angelo, 90
Gallo, 12, 89
  Cabernet, 19
  Ernest and Julio, 12
  Frei Ranch Zinfandel*, 71
  Sonoma Estate, 12
Gary Farrell, 13
  Merlot, 60
  Pinot Noir*, 49
Getty, Gordon, 30
Geyser Peak, 77
  Cabernet*, 19, 28
  Shiraz*, 78, 79
Gloria Ferrer
  Blanc de Noirs NV*, 97
  Pinot Noir, 44
Goldschmidt, Nick, 19
Grace Family, 13
Grahm, Randall, 13–14, 77, 96
Greenwood Ridge Pinot Noir*, 39, 49
Groom, Daryl, 19, 77
Groth, 23–24
  Merlot, 23–24
  Reserve, 17

Hanzell Pinot Noir, 42
Hartford Court
  Pinot Noir*, 39, 49
  Zinfandel*, 71
Hedges Cabernet, 27
Heitz, Alice and Joe, 24
Heitz Martha's Vineyard Cabernet, 17, 24
Henschke Shiraz, 82
Hess Cabernet*, 28
Hobbs, Paul, 13
Hogue Cellars, The
  Cabernet, 27
  Merlot*, 61
Horton Cellars Winery, 1
Howell Mountain
  Cabernet, 21–22
  Merlot, 59
Hunter Ashby Merlot*, 61

Il Podere dell'Olivos
  Barbera, 93
  Nebbiolo*, 92
Inglenook Cabernet, 25

Iron Horse, 3, 60, 101
  Cabernet, 33, 34
  Pinot Noir, 39, 40, 43
  Rosé, 96
  Sangiovese, 88
Italian varietals, 84–94. *See also specific wine*
Italy
  Barbera, 93
  comparison, California Sangiovese and Tuscan, 90
  Dolcetto, 93–94
  Merlot, 58, 64
  Nebbiolo, 92–93
  Sangiovese, 85, 87
  "super-Tuscans," 90

"J" Pinot Noir, 44
Jackson, Jess, 19
Jade Mountain Pinot Noir, 27, 43
Jefferson, Thomas, 6–7, 16, 75, 84
Jekel, Bill, 35
Jensen, Josh, 43–44
  Pinot Noir, 44
Jordan Cabernet, 17, 19
Joseph Phelps
  Cabernet, 24
  Rosé*, 96, 97
  Syrah*, 77, 79
Joseph Swan Pinot Noir, 40, 42
J. Rochioli Pinot Noir*, 40, 43, 49

Kathryn Kennedy Cabernet, 26
Kendall Jackson, 13
  Cabernet, 19
Kent Rasmussen Dolcetto, 94
Kenwood, 20–21
  Cabernet, 20
  Zinfandel, 21
King Estate Pinot Noir, 48
Knight's Valley, 12
Kunde Estate Merlot*, 61

La Crema Pinot Noir*, 49
Laurel Glen, 19–20
  Terra Rosa Cabernet*, 20, 28
Leonetti Cellar
  Cabernet, 29
  Merlot, 62, 66
  Sangiovese, 89
Lewis, Randy, 13
Limerick Lane Cellars Zinfandel*, 71
Long, Zelma, 19
Louis M. Martini
  Cabernet*, 21, 28
  Merlot*, 61
  Monte Rosso Vineyard, 21
Lynch, Kermit, 6

Mahoney, Francis, 40
Marilyn Merlot, 59
Marimar Pinot Noir, 39
Marinus Cabernet, 27
Markham Merlot, 60
Martini, Louis M., Jr., 21, 58. *See also* Louis M. Martini
Martini, Michael, 21

Martinelli
  and J. Fritz Zinfandel, 68–69
  Pinot Noir, 40
Matanzas Creek
  Cabernet, 25
  Journey Merlot, 59
  Merlot*, 59, 60, 61
May, Martha and Tom, 24
Mazzei, Fillipo, 84
McDowell Valley
  Grenache Rosé*, 97
  Syrah*, 78, 79, 80
Mendocino, 39, 76, 78, 88
Merlot, 3
  aging, 59
  Andrew Will*, 61, 62
  Apex, 62
  Arrowood, 3
  Avignonesi (Italian), 64
  Benziger*, 61
  Beringer*, 59, 61
  Blackstone*, 61
  blends vs. 100%, 58–59
  Bordeaux and, 62–63
  Bulgarian, 58
  Canoe Ridge*, 61
  Castello di Ama, 64
  Chateau Ste. Michelle, 62
  Columbia Crest*, 57, 61
  Columbia Milestone, 62
  Columbia Signature Series*, 61
  Duckhorn*, 59, 60, 61, 64
  Estancia*, 61
  Ferrari-Carano*, 61
  food and, 65–66
  grapes, imported, 57–58
  Groth, 23–24
  Hogue, The*, 61
  Howell Mountain, 59
  Hunter Ashby*, 61
  Italian, 58
  Journey, Matanzas Creek, 59
  Kunde Estate*, 61
  Leonetti, 62, 66
  Louis M. Martini*, 61
  Marilyn Merlot, 59
  Matanzas Creek*, 50, 61
  personal recommendations, 61
  prices, 57, 59, 60
  Pride*, 61
  St. Francis*, 60, 61
  Sebastiani*, 61
  Shafer*, 59, 60, 61
  Silverado*, 61
  Sinskey*, 60, 61
  Swanson*, 61
  Truchard*, 60, 61
  vintage chart, 64–65
  Washington State, 57, 60, 62, 63, 64
  Waterbrook*, 61
  when to drink, 63
  Whitehall Lane*, 61
  Woodward Canyon, 62
Meyer, Justin, 18
Mondavi
  Barbera, 93
  Cabernet, 17, 25, 30
  La Famiglia di Robert Mondavi, 89
  Luce, 89
  Reserve, 17, 23
Mondavi, Tim and Holly, 25
Mondavi, Robert, 87

Monterey County, 27, 35, 78
Monterey Cabernet, 25
Moueix, Christian, 25, 63
Mount Eden Cabernet, 26
Murphy-Goode Cabernet, 19
  Reserve*, 28

Napa, 78, 79, 87, 88
  Valley, 18, 21–26, 33, 44, 59
Napanook Cabernet, 25
Nebbiolo, 92–93
  food and, 93
  Il Podere dell'Olivos, 92
  Sanford, 92
  Seghesio, 92
  when to drink, 93
Niebaum-Coppola Estate Winery, 13

Opus One Cabernet, 17, 23, 25, 30
Oregon wine, 1, 2
  Pinot Noir, 39, 45–49
  vintages, 47, 53
  Zinfandel, 70
Ornellaia Sangiovese, 90

Palmer Vineyards, 1
Paris tasting, 1976, 16–17
Parker, Robert, 29, 69
Paul Thomas Pinot Noir, 47–48
Penfolds Winery, 77
  Shiraz, 82
Pepi, Robert, 85
Peterson, Dick, 25
Peterson, Joel, 68
Petite Sirah, 6. *See also* Syrah
  Christopher Creek, 79
  Fife*, 79
  Foppiano*, 79
  Hop Kiln, 79
  Russian River, 79
  Sonoma, 78–79
  Turley*, 77, 79
Peynaud, Emil, 87
Peyraud, Jean-Marie, 6
Pezzi-King Zinfandel*, 71
Philip Staley Syrah, 78
Pine Ridge
  Cabernet, 22
  Merlot, 60
Pinot Noir, 3, 6, 39
  Acacia*, 40, 43, 49
  Adelsheim, 48
  Archery Summit, 47, 48
  Au Bon Climat, 42, 43
  Beaux Frères, 45, 47, 48
  Bien Nacido, 41
  Brick House, 47
  Byron*, 49
  Calera, 43
  Carneros Creek, 40
  Central Coast, 41–42
  Chalone, 42
  comparisons with Burgundy, 49–51, 55
  Cristom's Marjorie and Mount Jefferson, 48
  Dehlinger*, 40, 49
  Domaine Carneros, 44
  Domaine Drouhin's Laurene, 47
  El Molino, 44
  Etude, 43

Flowers, 41
food and, 55-56, 91
Gary Farrell*, 49
Gloria Ferrer, 44
grape, 38-39
Greenwood Ridge*, 39, 49
Hanzell, 42
Hartford Court*, 39, 49
Iron Horse, 39, 40, 43
"J," 44
Jensen, 44
Joseph Swan, 40, 42
J. Rochioli*, 40, 43, 49
King Estate, 48
La Crema*, 49
Marimar, 39
Martinelli, 40
Napa Ridge*, 49
Oregon, 39, 45-49
Paul Thomas, 47-48
personal recommendations, 49
Ponzi's 25th Anniversary Reserve, 48
Reed, 44
Russian River, 40, 47
St. Innocent, 47
St. Innocent's Freedom Hill, 48
Saintsbury, 40, 43
Saintsbury Garnet* and Reserve*, 49
Sanford*, 41, 49
Sebastopol, 44
Selleck, 44
Sinskey*, 40, 43, 49
Sokol Blosser, 47
Steele, 43
vintage, breakthrough, 40, 52
vintage chart, 52-54
when to drink, 55
Williams Selyem*, 44-45, 49
Ponzi Pinot Noir, 48
Preston Estate Syrah, 78
Preston, Lou, 78
Pride Mountain
Cabernet*, 28
Merlot*, 61

Quilcida Creek, 29
Quivira Zinfandel*, 71
Qupé Syrah*, 79, 80

Rabbit Ridge Zinfandel*, 71
Rafanelli, Dave, 70
Ramey, Dave, 25
Ravenswood Zinfandel, 21, 68
Monte Rosso*, 71
Old Hill Ranch*, 71
Red Mountain Cabernet, 27
Red wine, about, 4-11
chaptalize or *soleil dans un sac*, 46
custom crush wines, 26
fining, 46
terroir, 11, 47, 87
unfiltered, 46
when to drink, 7-8
yeast, 45-46
young, 7-8, 55, 75
Reed Pinot Noir, 44
Renwood Zinfandel*, 71

Rhône, France, 75–76
Le Tresor grapes, 78
Marcel Guigal Côte Rôtie Syrah, 81–82
Syrah wines of, 80–82
R. H. Phillips "EXP" Syrah*, 79
Ridge Monte Bello Cabernet, 26
Ridge Vineyards, 102
Geyserville Zinfandel*, 71
Zinfandel, 68
Rocchetta, della, Mario Incisa, 87
Rodney Strong Cabernet*, 28
Rombauer Cabernet, 26
Rombauer, Irma, 26
Rosés, 95–99
Beringer, 96
Blanc de Pinot Noir, 95
Bonny Doon*, 96, 97
Domaine Chandon*, 97
Etude*, 95, 97
food and, 98–99
Gloria Ferrer*, 97
Iron Horse, 96
Joseph Phelps*, 96, 97
McDowell Valley*, 97
Pedroncelli, 96
Rosato di Sangiovese, 96
Saintsbury*, 95, 97
Sanford, 95
Simi, 95
sparkling, 96–97
Sutter Home, 96
Swanson*, 96, 97
when to drink, 97
Woodbridge, 96
Zinfandel, white, 96
Rosenblum, Kent, 68
Rosenblum Zinfandel, 68
Rossa, di, Rene, 40
Rutherford Cabernet, 22

St. Francis Merlot*, 60, 61
St. Innocent, 47
Freedom Hill Pinot Noir, 48
Saintsbury
Pinot Noir*, 40, 43, 49
Vincent Vin Gris Rosé*, 95, 97
Sanford
Nebbiolo*, 92
Pinot Noir*, 41, 49
Rosé, 95
Sanford, Richard, 41
Sangiovese, 85–86
Acorn*, 89
Atlas Peak, 87–88, 89
blending, 88
Bonny Doon*, 89
Chappellet*, 88, 89
Clos du Val*, 89
comparison, Tuscan wine, 90
Dalla Valle*, 89
Ferrari-Carano*, 88, 89
Flora Springs*, 89
food and, 91–92
regions growing, 88–90
Sassicaia, Tuscany, 87
Shafer Firebreak*, 88, 89
Staglin Stagliano*, 89
Swanson*, 89

Tignanello, 87
vintages, 90
when to drink, 90
Santa Barbara, 39, 41, 80
Santa Cruz, 26, 80
Sassicaia Sangiovese, 87
Sausal Zinfandel*, 71
Sbragia, Ed, 12
Screaming Eagle Cabernet, 13, 24–25
Sebastiani, Samuele, 84
Sebastiani Vineyards, 84
Barbera, 93
Merlot*, 61
Sebastopol Pinot Noir, 44
Seghesio
Barbera, 93
Nebbiolo*, 92
Zinfandel*, 71
Selleck Pinot Noir, 44
Selyem, Ed, 44
Shafer
Firebreak Sangiovese*, 88, 89
Hillside Cabernet, 22
Merlot*, 59, 60, 61
Shiraz, 76, 77, 82
Clarendon Hill, 82
Henschke and Co., 82
Penfolds, 82
Sierra Nevada foothills, 78, 80, 88
Sierra Vista Syrah, 80
Silver Oak Cabernet, 17, 18, 30, 33
Silverado
Cabernet, 22
Merlot*, 61
Simi Winery, 19
Reserve Cabernet*, 28
Rosé, 95
Simmons, Jean, 21
Sinskey (Robert)
Merlot*, 60, 61
Pinot Noir*, 40, 43, 49
Sokol Blosser Pinot Noir, 47
Solaia Sangiovese, 90
Sonoma, 12, 17, 33, 52, 53, 78, 84
Coast, 39, 40–41
Dry Creek Valley, 70, 72, 77, 78
Green Valley, 39, 60
Mountain, 19–20
Russian River, 39, 40, 78
Valley, 20
Sonoma Winery Pinot Noir, 42
Soter, Tony, 13, 43
Sparkling Wines, 44, 96–97, 98
Spottswoode Cabernet*, 13, 28
Staglin
Cabernet, 22, 23
Stagliano*, 89
Stag's Leap Cabernet, 16, 17, 22
Cask 23, 17, 22
Steele (Jed), 13, 39
DuPratt Zinfandel*, 71
Pinot Noir, 43
Steinhauer, Robert, 12
Strong, Rodney, 42
Sutter Home white Zinfandel, 96

Swan, Joe, 42
Swanson
  Cabernet, 24
  Merlot*, 61
  Rosato*, 96, 97
  Sangiovese*, 89
  Syrah, 79–80
Syrah. *See also* Petite Sirah
  Australian, 76, 82
  blends, 75, 78, 82
  Bonny Doon*, 79, 80
  comparisons with France and Australia, 80–82
  Dehlinger, 78
  Eberle*, 79, 80
  Edmunds St. John, 80
  Fetzer's Bonterra Syrah, 78
  food and, 82–83
  Forest Glen Shiraz*, 79
  Foxen*, 79
  French, 75–76, 80–82
  Geyser Peak Shiraz*, 78, 79
  grape, 75–78
  growing regions, 77–78, 80
  Joseph Phelps*, 77, 79
  McDowell Valley*, 78, 79, 80
  personal recommendations, 79
  Petite Sirah and, 76
  Preston, 78
  Qupé*, 79, 80
  R. H. Phillips "EXP"*, 79
  Sierra Vista, 80
  Staley, 78
  Swanson, 79–80
  Tepusquet, 80
  Thackery's Orion, 80
  Toad Hollow, 78
  vintages, Sonoma, 78
  when to drink, 80
  Zaca Mesa*, 79, 80

Tancer, Forrest, 3, 38, 42, 44, 86, 88, 95
T-bar-T Cabernet, 18
Tchelistcheff, André, 22, 23
Tepusquet Syrah, 80
Thackery's Orion Syrah, 80
Toad Hollow Syrah, 78
Truchard Merlot*, 60, 61
Turley
  Petite Sirah*, 77, 79
  Zinfandel, 68
Turley, Helen, 13, 69
Turley, Larry, 68

Viader Vineyards, 13
Vineyard 29, 13
Vineyards, 9, 11, 12–14, 18. *See locations; vineyard names*
Vintage charts
  Cabernet, 33–35
  Bordeaux, 9
  importance of, 9
  Merlot, 64–65
  Pinot Noir, 52–54
  Sangiovese, 90
  Zinfandel, 72–73

Washington State wine, 1
  Cabernets, 27–29
  Merlot, 27–28, 57, 60–62, 63, 64–65
  Sangiovese, 89–90

Waterbrook Merlot*, 61
Wendt, Henry, 102
White wines, 4, 5
Whitehall Lane
  Cabernet*, 22, 28
  Leonardini Merlot*, 61
Willamette Valley, 39, 48
Williams, Burt, 44, 53
Williams, Craig, 79
Williams Selyem Pinot Noir, 44–45
Winery Lake Pinot Noir, 40
Woodbridge (Mondavi) white Zinfandel, 96
Woodward Canyon
  Cabernet, 29
  Merlot, 62

Zaca Mesa "Z" Cuvée Syrah*, 79, 80
Zellerbach, James, 42
Zinfandel, 67–74, 102
  A. Rafanelli*, 71
  Biale, 69
  Bannister*, 71
  Chateau Potelle*, 71
  Cline*, 71
  Clos du Val, 71
  DeLoach*, 71
  Fife Redhead Zin*, 71
  Gallo Frei Ranch*, 71
  Hartford Court*, 71
  Kenwood Vineyards, 21
  Limerick Lane*, 71
  Martinelli and J. Fritz, 68–69
  old vine, 69–70
  personal recommendations, 71
  Pezzi-King*, 71
  price, 70
  Rafanelli, 70
  Ravenswood, 21, 68
  Ravenswood's Monte Rosso* and Old Hill Ranch*, 71
  Renwood*, 71
  Ridge, 68
  Ridge Geyersville*, 71
  Rosenblum, 68
  Sausal*, 71
  Seghesio*, 71
  Steele's DuPratt*, 71
  trend in, 71, 73
  Turley, 68
  vintage chart, 72–73
  when to drink, 73
Zinfandel Advocates and Producers (ZAP), 67–68